Catherine Labouré

AND THE MODERN

APPARITIONS OF OUR LADY

Catherine Labouré

AND THE MODERN
APPARITIONS OF OUR LADY

BY

OMER ENGLEBERT

Translated from the French by
ALASTAIR GUINAN

P. J. KENEDY & SONS

NEW YORK

1090

Nihil Obstat: Edward J. Montano, S.T.D.
Censor Librorum
Imprimatur: ✠ Francis Cardinal Spellman
Archbishop of New York

New York
December 30, 1958

Library of Congress Catalogue Card Number: 59–5564

Copyright © 1959 by P. J. Kenedy & Sons, New York

PRINTED IN THE UNITED STATES OF AMERICA

This work is based on the following sources: M. Aladel, C.M., *Notice historique sur l'origine et les effets de la Médaille Miraculeuse*, 8 editions, Paris, 1834 to 1842; M. Chevalier, C.M., *La Médaille Miraculeuse, origine, histoire, diffusion*, 3 editions, Paris, 1878–1895; Edmond Crapez, C.M., *La vénérable Catherine Labouré*, 6th ed., Paris, 1913; *Annales de la Congrégation de la Mission (Lazaristes) et de la compagnie des Filles de la Charité*, t. 95, n. 378, Paris 1930, pp. 453–554; Lucien Misermont, C.M., *La bienheureuse Catherine Labouré et la Médaille miraculeuse, documents, aperçu critique*, 3ème éd., Paris, 1933; *L'âme de la bienheureuse Catherine Labouré et quelques circonstances moins connues des Apparitions de la Médaille miraculeuse*, Paris 1933.

These works embody the substance of the saint's own writings about the visions, the testimony of her confessors, the principal points brought out by the several ecclesiastical inquiries, and other trustworthy information which could be gathered together.

CONTENTS

Part One

CATHERINE LABOURÉ

AND THE

MIRACULOUS MEDAL

1

The Childhood and Youth of
Catherine Labouré
(1806–1830)

THE SAINT who received the revelation of the Miraculous Medal was born at Fain-les-Moutiers (Côte-d'Or, France) at about six o'clock on the evening of May 2, 1806. Although her name was entered on the civil register of births as Catherine, and this was also the name given her in baptism, so long as she remained in the world she was known as Zoé, probably because her birthday is the feast of that saint. When Catherine Labouré began her religious life she resumed her baptismal name.

Fain-les-Moutiers, then as now, numbered about two hundred inhabitants, and nestled among trees on a plain. This small agricultural district is about two miles from Moutiers-Saint-Jean which, hardly more populous, takes its name from the monastery founded by St. Jean de Réomé who died in 554. Well known in its time, it was wholly destroyed during the French Revolution, and is now but a heap of ruins.

The story goes that Clovis, king of the Franks, offered to Jean de Réomé all the land that he could cover in one day's travel while mounted on his donkey. If this tradition be true, we must conclude that the beast went along at a good pace, for the abbey was the possessor of vast terri-

1

torial holdings. One was the village of Fain, and to indicate its dependency on the abbey the old word "Moutiers" (deriving from the Latin *monasterium*) was made part of its name.

The land is the land of Burgundy, a place renowned for noble wines, but even more celebrated for spiritual riches: it is one of those corners of the world in which God seems to have dowered men very plentifully with his best gifts. Here have arisen many men remarkable for intellect or holiness, many famed for creative genius in the arts. The little town of Dijon alone, which is quite near Fain, is the birthplace of at least five whose fame is world wide: Rameau the musician, the sculptor Rude, Bossuet, St. Bernard and the foundress of the Visitation Nuns, St. Jeanne de Chantal. Great works of art abound in Burgundy. Here are found churches in both Romanesque and Gothic styles, together with paintings, sculptures, monuments and art objects of every kind. From the religious point of view, thought of Burgundy evokes at once the name of Cluny, that nursery of popes, which during the Middle Ages numbered more than two thousand abbeys among its dependencies; of Citeaux, the cradle of Cistercians and of Trappists; of Paray-le-Monial, whence came the modern devotion to the Sacred Heart.

Our saint, therefore, was born in a place whereon the Spirit of God has been pleased to breathe.

Pierre Labouré, Catherine's father, and her mother, Madeleine Gontard, were members of the higher class of the peasantry. Pierre, who was born in 1767, was the owner of a fine farm. He had at one time felt called to the priesthood, and had actually made some studies in a seminary. For a time he had served as mayor of Fain-les-Moutiers. His wife, Madeleine Gontard, who was born in 1770, came of a family of the minor provincial nobility. A woman who joined some intellectual distinction to a religious temperament, she had been a teacher in her youth. She was married to Pierre Labouré on June 4, 1793, and bore him seventeen children of whom but ten survived.

Six boys and one girl were living when Catherine came into the world. Two more children were to arrive later: Tonine was born in 1808 and Auguste in 1809. We shall often encounter Tonine in our story. We shall speak also of Hubert, born in 1794, who was an officer in the armies of Napoleon and later a police commandant; of Marie-Louise, born in 1795, who entered a convent, left it, and re-entered; of Charles, born in 1800, who was a restaurateur at Paris.

There was no school for girls at Fain. The nearest one was at Moutiers-Saint-Jean, but this was too far for Catherine to travel. Therefore, she did not go to classes, with the result that she was twenty-three before she learned to read and write. She never mastered spelling, and what writings of hers we have bristle with errors; she wrote as she pronounced.

When, on October 9, 1815, death called the mother of this family of ten, several of the older children had already left the paternal home. Her mother's death was a great sorrow for Catherine, who was then aged nine and a half.

Tonine tells us: "At this time there was a figure of Our Lady atop a high wardrobe in our parents' room. One day, shortly after my mother's death, the servant of the house found my sister there, perched upon a table which she had pushed close to the wardrobe. Clasping the statue in her arms, she was tearfully begging the Virgin to take the place of the mother we had lost by herself becoming our Mother."

Pierre Labouré was disconsolate, feeling indeed beside himself at the death of his beloved wife and perfect companion. Already autocratic and a little harsh in his manner, he seems to have become more difficult. This would explain why of all his sons Auguste alone — and he was in poor health — remained at home with him. The others had all betaken themselves to Paris.

Pierre entrusted the household to Marie-Louise, then aged twenty, and sent Catherine and Tonine to be cared for by his sister at Saint-Rémy. She was married to a vinegar merchant called Jeanrot, and was herself the mother of four little girls. In this small village, nine miles from Fain, where the château of St. Bernard's uncles still stands, the two orphan girls spent the years 1816 and 1817 and were educated with their cousins in a religious atmosphere. Sixty-five years later, one of them was to testify at the ecclesiastical inquiry into Catherine's holiness that at that early date she was already exemplary in her behavior.

At the beginning of 1818 Pierre Labouré came for his two children and brought them home with him. The time had come for the elder to make her first Communion, and she did this in the church of Moutiers-Saint-Jean on January 25, 1818. Tonine says of Catherine: "My sister impressed everyone with her fervor, and later she told me that on that day she had made up her mind that like Marie-Louise, our big sister, she too would consecrate herself to God."

As a matter of fact, Marie-Louise entered the Convent of the Daughters of Charity two months later. Catherine rejoiced in her sister's happiness, and wishing her to have no regrets about leaving home assured her that she was well able to take her place in directing the household. Pointing to Tonine, she said to her father: "We two are quite well able to keep house." She was only twelve years old, and Tonine scarcely ten, yet events showed that she had not been presumptuous, for during the following ten years she indeed kept the house going well. All the evidence produced at the inquiries preceding her beatification proves this.[1]

One witness declared: "From the day after her first Communion, she gave herself up entirely to work, she accustomed herself to fatigue, she established herself in habits of orderliness and initiative. She was only fourteen when the single household servant the Labourés had, decided to leave her place in order to get married. It was Catherine who insisted that no one else be hired, and the two sisters added the servant's duties to their own."

Together they kept house, cooked the meals, did the washing and mending, took care of the poultry bins, the stables and the garden. "In summertime, Catherine carried her father's lunch to him wherever he might be working in the fields in the company of a dozen hired hands."

In the yard of the farmhouse the large dovecote with its great tower sheltered between seven and eight hundred pigeons. "My sister it was who usually took care of feeding these birds," said Tonine. "They would fly to her, circling about her head, getting caught in her hair and sitting on her shoulders. She would pause happily in the midst of them, and it made a charming picture to see her there." Her brothers recalled that "she did all things well and

---

[1] These inquiries are of two kinds; one is termed "Ordinary" and is under the direction of the bishops of the diocese in which the subject has lived; the other inquiry is made at the Roman Court and is termed "Apostolic."

quickly," and that it was "but rarely that our father, despite his natural severity, had even a slight reproach for her."

At the inquiry a woman of eighty who had known the sisters when she was a child declared: "What examples those girls were! They were admired as perfect house-wives. They took no part in worldly amusements and only went out to help the villagers or to attend services in the church. I can see them now as on Sunday after Mass they would bid a pleasant good day to young girls of their own age as they left the church, and then would hasten home-ward where their household duties awaited them."

Catherine's life was a life of work from her twelfth to her twenty-second year.

Catherine passed through the period of adolescence without being troubled or upset. Tonine tells us that "in all things where evil was concerned she was quite direct and innocent." Her imagination and her thoughts were never occupied with fleshly desires, and she kept her child-like innocence of mind and body to the end of her life. Already, at this time, her true piety was remarked.

As there was no resident priest at Fain, it was the pastor of the parish of Moutiers-Saint-Jean who attended to the spiritual needs of the villagers and who came on Sundays to say Mass for them. Other religious services were held at Moutiers where, in addition to the parish church, there was a house of the Daughters of Charity to which a chapel was attached.

Catherine was not satisfied with going every after-noon to pray in the church of Fain where her family had their own private oratory in a recess to the left of the high altar. She would arise before dawn several times a week so that she might go to Moutiers to hear Mass, sometimes in the parish church, at others in the Sisters' chapel.

It was her attitude while at prayer that most impressed those who saw her. She had no use for benches or cushions, and in winter as well as in summer knelt on the uncovered pavement. Here she remained immovable and as though transfixed, her eyes upon the tabernacle. "One would have taken her to be an angel," the witnesses at the inquiry afterward declared. It was at this time that she contracted the arthritis of the knees of which she was never cured.

We finally learn that from the age of fourteen she fasted in secret on Fridays and on Saturdays. When Tonine discovered this and threatened to tell their father, Catherine replied: "Very well, go ahead." Pierre Labouré pressed her to cease her fasting; finding her set upon continuing and yet not impaired in health, he gave up the attempt.

"She was already a mystic," says Tonine.

The word is well chosen but it should be explained, for in it lies the key to our saint's life.

The mystic is one attuned to mystery. For such a one the invisible world is more present and real than the outer world that surrounds us. In this inner region the mystic seems to move sure-footedly, while others find their way only by faith and at the cost of much effort, whereas certain others, such as the materialists, become wholly lost.

The soul of the mystic is attuned to God and to His saints, and it is with them that it holds converse. In this state it is indeed as an interchange that prayer is conceived of, so that what to many is a labored monologue becomes for the mystic a dialogue. So great is the soul's absorption in prayer that the mystic seems to be rapt out of himself when he prays; it appears as if he were hearing what he had listened for, as if he were seeing what he had sought.

This wondrous gift is far from being of the same nature as are the gifts of the speculative intellect, nor is it to be measured by them. It might better be compared to the artistic gifts of privileged genius, for example to the faculty of a musician who hears what he describes as harmony from heaven, music to which he alone is perceptive and which he alone can note down and develop.

Catherine was not at all gifted in the field of the speculative intellect, she was even less endowed in respect to imagination, originality of mind, literary or artistic sensitivity. She was, however, withdrawn and thoughtful; she possessed judgment and good sense; and, above all, she was the recipient of special insights which came to her as a result of prayer.

There is no doubt that the chief of the graces given her was this aptitude, this capacity, to feel and to savor the realities of the supernatural world. Yet another grace must be taken into account, for without it the first might have been less advantageous to her: this second grace was that she was born at Fain-les-Moutiers and that she passed her childhood there.

Just as is true of God's other gifts, it is true of the mystical capacity that it can grow or decrease or even disappear entirely. Greed, impurity, ambition, absorption in unworthy pleasure may account for its loss, while its lasting growth can be ascribed to renunciation, humility, recollection and faithfulness in prayer.

What might have become of Catherine had she been placed in surroundings dominated by the search for mere pleasure and the love of money? What if she had spent her days, from morning until evening, in a factory or in an office? What if her leisure had been divided between hurrying hither, thither and yon and the reading of silly trash, or between day-dreaming by the fireside and plunging into chattering and ceaseless exercise of the voice? Would not her soul have succumbed to such influences? Would it not have fallen into the poor, ordinary pattern, its own characteristics being stamped out and annihilated?

Fain-les-Moutiers, nestling among its trees, moved according to the rhythm of Nature, not to that of the machine. There time was taken for eating, for sleeping, for talking or for being silent. There was a time for thought and for listening, time to tend the garden, to play with the pigeons, to see the sun set, and to pray to God. There was not much bad example to be seen: evil hid itself and was called by its right name. Money did not usurp the place of God, and spiritual values were accorded the first place, which the Gospel says they should have. It was not felt at Fain-les-Moutiers that individuality should be suppressed; there was freedom for each to follow his bent. A soul permeated by a sense of the inner life could find opportunity for reflection; no one was required to submerge his true nature in a banal conformity. In a word, at Fain-les-Moutiers, a mystic such as Catherine found opportunity to hasten to the confrontation with God to which He was pleased to lead her.

Her chestnut hair, her lovely eyes and her noble face, as well as the fact that she was known to be a virtuous and healthy girl, attracted suitors who wished to marry her. When her father first spoke to her of such an offer, she told him what Tonine had known for a long while, "that she was betrothed to Jesus alone, and that He alone would be her spouse."

At least twice her father returned to the charge, but met with no greater success, despite the fact that the offers which were made had come from men who were worthy and honorable. It seems that Pierre Labouré did not really resent her refusals. Tonine would soon be twenty years old and might marry young; he was himself about sixty, and he may have cherished the notion that Catherine, by remaining a spinster, would be someone on whom he might lean in his old age.

However, when she told him, on attaining her majority, of her intention to enter the religious life, he became annoyed. He had his own notions about the rights of God and the duties of children. He thought that since he had three daughters it was all very well that one had dedicated herself to God, but he felt that the others should seek their happiness in the world.

Conditions at home became so difficult and so strained that a change became imperative and Pierre Labouré hit upon the idea that Catherine should make a visit to Paris. He expected her to return fully cured of unreasonable notions.

There were five of the sons of old Labouré at Paris: Jacques was a wine merchant, Joseph was in the business of glass bottles, Antoine was a pharmacist, Pierre was a clerk, Charles operated a restaurant. Charles had early lost his wife, and it was to his house that Catherine went in the autumn of 1828. The restaurant in which she began to work was at No. 20, Rue de l'Echiquier, in the district of Notre Dame de la Bonne Nouvelle, where many building projects were under way at the time. The place was frequented by workmen; it was a sort of "bistro" as we would call it nowadays. Charles had worked out an agreement with one of the important construction firms, and he supplied meals for the masons, carpenters, painters, pavers, and other workers employed by the firm.

Catherine did her best to wait on all these in an atmosphere compounded of cheap wine, tobacco fumes, musty onion soup, vulgar talk and swearing. She remained here for some months in a state of great unhappiness, but even more resolute than ever in her determination to follow her vocation to the religious life.

At about this time, or a little earlier, she seems to have had a dream which was a source of much comfort to her in her troubles with her father. Toward the end of her life she spoke of it to her sister, Marie-Louise:

"I dreamed that I was at prayer in our own little oratory in the church at Fain. I was alone in the church. Suddenly there came forth from the sacristy a white-haired priest, vested for Mass and carrying his chalice. He walked solemnly toward the altar, but as he passed by me he turned his head and looked fixedly at me with eyes which, although full of goodness, gleamed like fire. This shook me to the depths of my being.

"Mass began. Now, every time that he turned to say *Dominus vobiscum,* this old man looked at me so searchingly that I was unable to bear it. When he finished saying Mass he returned to the sacristy where he remained for a few minutes to unvest. Then I saw him again at the door, and he beckoned to me to come forward. But I was so frightened that I fled at once.

"However, I was by no means rid of him, for as I was returning home I stopped to visit one of our sick friends to hear how she was, and whom did I see behind me but the self-same old priest! He had followed me. And this time he spoke to me, saying, 'My child, it is all very well

to visit the sick . . . but you are running away from me.
. . . Nevertheless, the day will come when you will be with
me, for God has plans for you. Do not forget this!'

"These words of the old priest marked the end of my
dream."

Catherine herself was unable to write, and it was no
doubt to Charles that she dictated the letters which now
reached her sister-in-law, the wife of Hubert Labouré, and
her own sister, Marie-Louise, who was at the time superior
of the Daughters of Charity at Castelsarrasin (Tarn-et-
Garonne). Madame Hubert Labouré, who was originally
Jeanne Gontard and a blood cousin of her husband, was
the proprietress of a pensionnat or boarding school for
young girls at Châtillon-sur-Seine (Côte-d'Or), about
thirty miles from Fain-les-Moutiers.

In her reply to Catherine's letter, Marie-Louise congratulated her sister on her vocation and encouraged her
to persevere: "You tell me that you wish you were already tasting the happiness of the religious life, but remember this: if God is calling you, there is no one who
can stop you from responding to your vocation."

She went on to advise Catherine very strongly to fix
her choice on the congregation of the Daughters of Charity, and she closed her letter with these words: "I join
with our dear sister-in-law in her suggestion that you visit
her. Whatever may be the final outcome, it is certainly
needful that you improve your French, and that you learn
how to write and how to figure. . . ."

These lines indicate that it was Madame Hubert Labouré who had proposed the idea of receiving at her pensionnat the daughter who had been practically put out of

her father's house. This would enable her to escape from the unhappiness she felt in Paris.

Was it perhaps that Madame Hubert Labouré was the niece of his dear departed wife, and that she recalled to him her beauty and her goodness, that the obstinate Pierre Labouré agreed to hear of the plan? As we shall see, he returned to the matter twice during the following months. To begin with, he agreed that Catherine leave Paris and establish herself at Châtillon-sur-Seine. She arrived there, as it appears, in time for the reopening of classes in September 1829.

Madame Labouré's boarding school was situated in what had formerly been the house of a Carmelite community at No. 24, Rue Bourg-à-Mont. Certainly these were surroundings of greater distinction than those of the Parisian bistro, but it was all too much for Catherine.

The pupils were daughters of the Burgundian nobility, and to these charming damsels the dancing master came to teach the proper fashion of recovering a lace handkerchief which had fallen to the floor, how to hold a fan, how to offer sweets. The music master taught them the harp and the piano. They also studied mythology, Gautier's *Histoire de France en vers,* and they even dabbled in astronomy. . . .

Our unlettered farmwoman of twenty-three had no interest in either astronomy or mythology, and the dancing and the harp playing were alike unattractive to her. She grieved that she was not already in a convent. Catherine had little to do with the young ladies, for her sister-in-law housed her in her own quarters. However, this situation did not long endure, for at this time the old priest of her dream appeared again to call Catherine once more.

There was a convent of the Daughters of Charity at Châtillon-sur-Seine. They administered the *bureau de bienfaisance,* or charity center, which stood on the Rue de la Haute-Juiverie on the right bank of the river, and Jeanne Gontard persuaded her sister-in-law to go there to discuss her vocation with the Sisters.

Catherine knocked at the door. A Sister admitted her to the parlor. Here the very first thing she saw, among a number of edifying pictures hanging on the wall, was the likeness of the priest of her dreams! She asked who the saint was, and the Sister replied:

"That is our founder, St. Vincent de Paul."

The visit was the first of several, but before coming to a final decision, Catherine asked the advice of the Abbé Prost, the pastor of Châtillon-sur-Seine, who was her confessor.

He said to her: "My child, it must have been St. Vincent de Paul whom you saw in your dream, and I think that he is asking you to join the ranks of his daughters."

Catherine no longer hesitated as to what congregation she would enter. But it remained to obtain the agreement of her father, Pierre Labouré, and here again it was Jeanne Gontard who intervened and succeeded in winning his consent. He gave it but grudgingly, and in order to make it clear that he stood firm and unchanged in his own views, he declared that he would supply neither trousseau nor dowry.

At the *bureau de bienfaisance* Catherine had made a special friend in Sœur Victoire Séjolle who was charged with the duty of visiting the homes of the sick. It was to this religious that Catherine owed the permission which was given her to serve her postulancy at Châtillon-sur-

Seine, and she began this stage of her religious training on January 30, 1830.

Ordinarily, the postulancy lasts for three months. It is a sort of proving ground before entry is granted to the seminary or novitiate.[2] Its purpose is to confirm true vocations and to discern them from others. The postulant retains her secular dress, but lives among the Sisters, following their spiritual exercises and learning the nature of their work while yet remaining perfectly free to return to the world should she wish to do so.

A large portion of Catherine's postulancy was passed with Sœur Séjolle who taught her to read and write, giving to this task a half hour daily. She often took her with her when she visited the sick. Sœur Séjolle was one of two individuals who sensed that the newly arrived postulant was a privileged soul. The other who discerned this was an old servant at the institution called Mariette.

St. Vincent de Paul, in the Rule he gave to the Daughters of Charity, prescribed that "every day, at three o'clock, the Sisters shall fall upon their knees. Then one of them is to say aloud *Christus factus est* — 'Christ became obedient for us unto death, even unto the death of the Cross.' All shall thus adore the Son of God who died to save our souls by offering to the Eternal Father this moment at which He gave up the ghost, and by praying that the merits of His death may be applied to sinners in their agony and to the souls detained in Purgatory. Having so adored for the time of three *Paters* and *Aves*, they are to kiss the ground and rise at once."

Old Mariette had seen many things and many Sisters

2 The Sisters of Charity actually use the word séminaire or seminary in place of the term novitiate which is common in other congregations. (Trans.)

during her lifetime; she retained all her curiosity, and watched Catherine closely. She was struck by finding her always in the chapel at three o'clock. Mariette liked to recount that she had never heard any Sister say the prayer with so much indication of heart-felt devotion.

Sœur Séjolle, for her part, was not less impressed by the interior life of her twenty-three-year-old disciple. The next year, whenever she heard anything said of the apparitions in the Rue du Bac, she remarked: "If Our Lady has appeared to a novice in the seminary, it can be to none other than to Sœur Labouré, for to my mind this soul is destined to receive from heaven its very highest favors."

Later on, every time she went to Paris for the annual retreat, Sœur Séjolle made a point of visiting Catherine at the Hospice d'Enghien. She sent other Sisters to see her as well, and said: "I shall be dead, but you who will still be living will be happy to have been with this privileged friend of the Virgin Mary."

The three months of postulancy being over, it was time for Catherine to go to Paris to enter the seminary. Pierre Labouré obstinately persisting in his refusal to give Catherine anything for ten years during which she had worked for him, it was once again the charming and generous Jeanne Gontard who put together her trousseau and gave the required dowry. This latter was six hundred and seventy-two francs, a considerable amount at a time when the daily wages of a Burgundian laborer amounted to but twenty-five centimes.

As for Catherine's trousseau it comprised: "4 pair of bed sheets; 12 embroidered napkins; material for making chemises and 11 already made; 5 gowns of which 4 were of printed stuff and 1 of violet silk; 1 piece of cotton; 1

length of cotton; 30 headbands, 20 of which were to be made up; 11 pocket handkerchiefs; 5 pair of hose; 1 corset and 1 black gown."

Catherine seems not to have returned to Fain-les-Moutiers. Did her father perhaps refuse to allow her to say farewell to him? . . . She must have wept as she embraced Jeanne Gontard, who had been providentially sent to her during the most trying months of her life. She must have cried, too, over her dear Tonine who loved her so much and understood her so well, and with whom she had been so very happy.

Carrying the trunk that contained her trousseau, she climbed up into the coach with an old Sister who was at the point of retirement and was going to live at the motherhouse in the Rue du Bac.

"On April 21, 1830, it being the Wednesday before the day of the translation of St. Vincent's relics, I reached Paris," she wrote. "It seemed to me that I was walking on air, I was so happy."

2

Catherine at the Seminary — the First Apparitions (April–July, 1830)

THE RELIGIOUS COMMUNITY which Catherine now entered is one of two congregations founded by St. Vincent de Paul (1580–1660). The other is called the Congregation of Priests of the Mission or Lazarists.[1]

In collaboration with Madame Le Gras (1591–1660), a widowed noblewoman of Paris, St. Vincent founded the Daughters of Charity in 1633. Madame Le Gras became their first superior general, and she has been canonized under her maiden name, Louise de Marillac.

In the following words Vincent indicated to his sisterhood the essence and nature of their vocation: "The principal end for which God has called them and gathered them together," wrote Vincent, "is that they may honor Our Lord Jesus Christ as the source and the model of all charity serving Him both corporally and spiritually in the person of the sick, of children, of prisoners, and of the poor in general.

"It is therefore their chief aim to work for the poor.

"In order that they may cooperate in so holy a calling

[1] The latter foundation was established in 1625. The name *Lazarists* comes from the fact that their first establishment was in the Priory of Saint-Lazare in Paris. [In the United States, the Lazarists are commonly called Vincentians. Trans.]

they must resolutely cleave to holiness of life, and they must strive with the greatest care for their own perfection, joining interior devotion to the exterior works of charity."

He wrote also that "they must abhor the principles of worldliness and cleave to those of Jesus Christ, especially in all that concerns interior and exterior mortification; they must hold themselves and worldly things in contempt so that they will have no attachments to any created thing, neither to place, to kinds of work, nor to persons; and they must hold themselves in readiness to abandon whatever they may be doing when obedience requires it."

For her part, it was the wish of St. Louise de Marillac that her daughters be marked by "simplicity, cordiality and cheerfulness."

It is in the novitiate or seminary that the Daughter of Charity, wearing the religious habit and living apart from the world, is initiated into the spirit of her congregation. For between eight and twelve months, under experienced direction, she makes an effort to build up a strong interior life and to acquire the virtues necessary for her state.

The order of the day at the seminary was as follows:

4:00 — Rising, followed by prayer, meditation and Mass.

During the course of the morning each Sister is occupied with her assigned work; and "if a group works together they may converse upon some religious subject in a serious fashion and not as a form of recreation."

11:30 — Particular examen, luncheon, recreation.

2:00 — Spiritual reading, followed by the great silence.

3:00 — Act of adoration.

5:30 — Half-hour meditation in the chapel.

7:00 — Dinner, followed by recreation.

8:00 — The subject of the following day's meditation is read, night prayers, retire.

Furthermore, the Rule requires the daily recitation of the Rosary. St. Vincent wrote: "After your morning prayers, you are to say one decade, then two decades are to be said in chapel, a fourth decade should follow the midday Angelus, and the last decade is to be said after the evening Angelus."

In 1830 there were about one hundred fifty religious in residence in the motherhouse in the Rue du Bac; and it was here that the seminary was located. Nearby then, as now, was the motherhouse of the Lazarists in the Rue de Sèvres.

At the time of Catherine's arrival, the subject on which all minds and hearts were fixed at the Rue de Sèvres, as at the Rue du Bac, was the translation of the body of St. Vincent de Paul, set for the following Sunday. Forty years before the remains of their founder had been removed from the motherhouse of the Lazarists, so that they might be spared from profanation during the French Revolution.

Now, on April 30, 1830, the body was restored to St. Vincent's sons. It was carried in a magnificent procession from the metropolitan church of Notre Dame, across Paris, to the chapel on the Rue de Sèvres. Eight hundred Daughters of Charity were in the cortège. Among them was Catherine.

For the space of the novena or nine days' prayer of thanksgiving which followed the translation of the holy relics, Catherine went with the other novices of the seminary to pray daily in the chapel in the Rue de Sèvres.

It was at this time that there began the series of apparitions of Our Lady which were to bring us the Miraculous Medal.

The saint has herself written: "I asked of St. Vincent all the grace that I needed. I besought him as well for France and for our two families" (the Lazarists and the Daughters of Charity).

It grieved her to have to interrupt these prayers. "It gave me pain to leave Saint-Lazare (in the Rue de Sèvres); but I found St. Vincent, or at least his heart (in the Rue du Bac), and each time that I returned home it appeared to me. I had the sweet solace of seeing it above the little reliquary in the Sisters' chapel."

During the novena, this "little reliquary" was set upon a table at the right side of the high altar; here the novices continued their prayers after they returned from Saint-Lazare. The reliquary contained not only the saint's heart, but also a bone taken from one of his forearms.

"It (the heart of St. Vincent) appeared to me under three different forms, each time on three successive days:

"(On the first three days) I saw it as white, flesh color, bespeaking peace, calm, innocence and unity.

"(On the three following days) I saw it red as fire, as if to signify that charity which by enkindling all hearts could, as it seemed to me, bring renewal to the whole community (in both its branches) and cause it to spread throughout the world.

"(On the three final days) I saw it as dark red, and this filled me with sorrow. It brought me a sense of almost insurmountable sadness connected, I know not why or how, with some widespread change."

She later declared to M. Aladel that "an inner Voice told me that St. Vincent was deeply grieved by the disasters in store for France. On the ninth day, however, that Voice made me understand that he was somewhat consoled, having obtained assurance from God, through the intercession of Our Lady, that neither of his two families would perish, that God would rather make use of them to restore the Faith."

The name of M. Aladel (1800–1865) which we have just encountered is one which henceforth will recur constantly in our pages.[2] This man was a young Lazarist who served as confessor to the seminary Sisters. As events fell out, he was to stand revealed as a true man of God, a good psychologist and a prudent director of souls. But at this time he was only thirty years of age; he was distrustful of himself and more distrustful of the insignificant novice who, barely out of her village home, was already troubling him with tales of visions, prophecies and portents.

That she was not considered worthy of much attention is a fact established by the testimony of competent authority. As a matter of fact, this is how she was described in the official register of the community upon the completion of her seminary training:

"Catherine Labouré: Strong (she enjoys good health). Of middle height. Knows how to read and to write for her own use (that is to say, one would not like to show others her writing, so bizarre is her spelling). Her character seems good (let us hope reality will confirm this appearance). Neither in intelligence nor in judgment is she outstanding. She is devout. Tries to make progress in virtue."

M. Aladel severely cautioned his penitent, after he had

---

2 Secular priests in France, and even Sulpicians and Vincentians, are spoken of, and addressed, as Monsieur l'Abbé or just Monsieur. Only priests in religious orders (Jesuits, Dominicans, etc.) are called Father.

The same convenient distinction obtained in America until about the middle of the nineteenth century.

heard the things she told him, to remain calm and humble in her duties and put aside all dreams and fancies.

But how was she to do this?

It now became Our Lord Himself who repeatedly appeared to her.

"I was given another great grace: this was to see Our Lord in the most Blessed Sacrament, both at the time of Communion and during exposition (in the ostensorium). I saw Him all during my time in the seminary, save only when I doubted. The following time (that is, the time which followed that when I had been doubtful of the reality of the apparition) I saw nothing."

It is only in respect to one of these visions that we are supplied with details. This occurred on Trinity Sunday, June 6, 1830.

"On this day, Our Lord showed Himself to me in the Blessed Sacrament vested as a king, and adorned with the cross upon His breast. Then, a moment afterward, I saw Him without His regal ornaments; everything, including the cross, fell to the ground at His feet. "It was then that I was oppressed by the most sad thoughts.

"I believed, as a result of what I had seen, that the earthly King was to be dethroned and deprived of his royal ornaments; and all kinds of ideas, which I find it impossible to express, came to me about the evils that would follow."

One may conclude that had M. Aladel known of these visions he would not have placed any more faith in them than in those that had gone before. Nor would he have believed for an instant that "the earthly King," Charles X of France, was about to lose his crown and his throne.

A month and a half later, M. Aladel's penitent came

to him with the following story, one of the most charming in the entire history of the appearances of Our Lady during the nineteenth and twentieth centuries. The events with which it is concerned took place during the night of July 18–19, 1830. Catherine writes: "The feast of St. Vincent (July 19) was approaching. On the eve, our dear Mère Marthe (one of the novice mistresses) instructed us on the subject of devotion to the saints, and in particular on devotion to the Blessed Virgin.

"For how long a time had I wished to see the Blessed Virgin! My desire became even stronger, and I actually went to bed with the idea that on that very night I might see my dear Mother. We had each received from Mère Marthe a little scrap of the rochet of St. Vincent.[3] I cut mine in two and swallowed half before going to sleep, persuaded that St. Vincent would obtain for me the grace of seeing the Blessed Virgin."

No doubt this will make some people critical, even arouse them to laughter. "How eccentric and how unhygienic," they will say. But lest they look down upon Catherine, lest they lose a proper sense of humility, we may remark, in the first place, that it is better and more hygienic to swallow, once in a lifetime, a few linen threads than to absorb every day glass after glass of strong spirits; and further, that the scoffers themselves might swallow one or more whole relics without being favored either by their guardian angels or the Holy Virgin in the manner in which we shall see Catherine was favored.

The seminary Sisters slept in a common dormitory, each one having her own alcove surrounded by curtains.

"I was asleep," Catherine continues, "when at eleven-

---

[3] A vestment of linen similar to the surplice, but having fitted sleeves. — Trans.

thirty I heard my name: 'Sister, Sister, Sister Catherine!' said a voice.

"I looked toward the side from which the voice came. It was the side of the passage (on which the alcoves opened). I lifted my curtain and saw a child of about five or six, dressed completely in white. He said: 'Come with me to the chapel; the Blessed Virgin awaits you!'

"I thought at once that I should be overheard going. 'Do not be troubled,' said the child. 'It is half-past eleven and everyone is asleep. Come, I am waiting.'

"I dressed quickly and joined the child. I followed after him. He went on my left, and from him there came forth rays of light. To my great astonishment lights were shining brightly all along our way. But my astonishment increased when, as we approached the chapel, the door opened at a slight touch of the child's finger.

"My amazement was at its height as I then beheld all the candles and torches in the chapel lit in a way that reminded me of midnight Mass. However, I saw no sign of the Blessed Virgin.

"The child led me into the sanctuary to the side of the chaplain's chair (on the Gospel side). Here I knelt down while the child remained standing. All this while I was looking to see whether the Sisters on watch would pass through the sanctuary."

What would the Sisters who were keeping the night watch have thought if, on coming into the tribune on the Epistle side, they had found Catherine in the sanctuary at such an hour?

"Then a moment later, the child said: 'Here is the Blessed Virgin; here she is!

"I heard the rustling of a silken robe coming from the side of the sanctuary. The 'Lady' bowed before the tabernacle, and then she seated herself in M. Richenet's chair."

This armchair, used by M. Richenet (chaplain at that time), whenever he gave a conference to the Sisters, was similar to a chair in a painting of St. Anne in the choir.

"But the 'Lady' did not look like St. Anne.

" (Seeing that) I did not know how to behave, the Child spoke to me again: 'It is the Blessed Virgin!' I am not able to say why, but it still seemed to me that it was not she whom I saw. It was then that the voice of the child changed and took on the deeper tones of a man's voice. He spoke again, strongly (repeating his words for the third time).

"At this moment I rushed forward and knelt before the Blessed Virgin with my hands on her knees. I cannot express what I felt, but I am sure that this was the happiest moment of my life.

"The Blessed Virgin spoke to me of the manner in which I ought to behave toward my director (M. Aladel) and she also confided to me some things which I may not reveal. She told me also how to act in times of distress. Pointing with her left hand to the altar steps, she told me to come there to refresh my heart, and she said that it was there that I would find all needed solace. When I asked what was the meaning of what I had seen, she explained it to me completely.

"I do not know how much time went by. (Her going) was like that of a light which goes out. She disappeared like a shadow, as she had come. 'She has gone,' said the child who, throughout, had been standing in the same place. Together, we went back by the way we had come. He continued to walk at my left side and to light up the way.

"It is my belief that this child, so resplendent in miraculous light, was my guardian angel, and that he had made himself visible in order that I might see the Blessed Virgin, for sight of whom I had so prayed.

"When I returned to the dormitory it was two o'clock in the morning, for I heard the hour strike. I went back to bed; but I did not sleep again that night."

This is the end of the account which Catherine drew up for M. Aladel in 1856, in confirmation of what she had immediately told him orally at the time it happened.

If this written account makes no mention of what the Blessed Virgin had told Catherine, it is because Our Lady had forbidden these things to be revealed to anyone except Catherine's confessor. Had they been put down in writing there would have been the risk of such a revelation, since such a paper might have fallen into the wrong hands.

Some months before she died in 1876, Catherine added the following lines to what she had written in 1856, Our Lady herself having then given her permission to do so:

"My child, God wishes to entrust to you a mission. It will be the cause of great suffering to you, but you will surmount it with the thought that it will work to God's glory.

"You will know later what this mission is to be, and you will be troubled until you have told the one who is charged with your guidance. You will be contradicted; but do not fear, grace will be given to help you. Tell (M. Aladel) of what you have seen; once more, have confidence and do not fear. In your prayers inspiration will be given you.

"The times are very evil. Great misfortune will come to France: her throne will be overthrown! The whole world will be upset by evils of every kind. — The Blessed Virgin seemed very much grieved when she said this. — But come to the foot of this altar; grace awaits all, whether they be great or little, who ask for it fervently and with confidence.

"My child, I am pleased to shower grace upon your community, for I love it very much. Nevertheless, I am saddened to see that great abuses exist: the Rule is not well observed, regularity is lacking. In both families (among the Lazarists as well) there has been too great a relaxation. Tell this to your director, although he is not (yet) the superior. Then, in time, when he will be given charge of the community in a special way, he is to do all he possibly can to restore the Rule. Tell him this as from me. He is to guard against bad reading matter, against loss of time and against useless visiting. . . .

"When the Rule will be again kept in honor, another community will come to be joined to your own. This is not customary, but I also very much love (the Sisters of) this community, and (that is why) you are to say (as from me) that they are to be received. God will bless them and they will enjoy great peace. And thus (increased) your community will become very large.

"Indeed there will be great danger, and it will be thought that all is lost when the misfortunes (of which I tell you) begin to occur. But I shall be with you; have confidence; you will see that I shall come to your aid, for you are under the divine protection, and St. Vincent will watch also over his two families.

"It will not be as well, alas, with other religious houses wherein there will be many victims" — Our Lady wept when she said this. "There will also be victims among the clergy of Paris. The archbishop himself will die" — at these words she wept again. "The Cross will be insulted; blood will flow in the streets" — here the Blessed Virgin could speak no longer so great was her grief, and this was shown in her face.

Catherine asked when these evils would come about. "I asked this question silently, and I understood perfectly when Our Lady replied: 'In forty years.'"

It is natural to ask if anything came of the prophecies reported by the saint. Some of them concerned her religious community; others had to do with her country, France. Events bore all of them out.

The fulfillment of the first group is seen in the life of a man who is regarded as being providentially "the second founder of St. Vincent de Paul's two congregations." This is M. Étienne who was named superior general in 1843. With the aid of M. Aladel, his friend and assistant, he put to rights all that needed adjustment in both communities, and they prospered increasingly thereafter.

The Lazarists multiplied and sent thousands of missionaries to pagan countries. A good number of these shed their blood for the Faith, and some have been raised to the altars of the Church.

For its part, the congregation of the Daughters of Charity, of which M. Aladel became director general, saw vocations increase to such an extent that it surpassed in numbers all other communities, and today it counts over forty thousand members.

Our Lady promised that another community would unite itself to the Daughters of Charity after the re-establishment of the observance of the Rule. Not only one, but three communities did so during the ten years following on the opening of M. Étienne's term of office. These are the Sisters of Elizabeth Seton (United States) in 1849, the Sisters of Leopoldine de Brandis (Austria) in 1851, and the Sisters of Charity of Verviers (Belgium) in 1854.[4]

As to the prophecies concerning the future of France, some were fulfilled in a very brief time; others dealt with a more distant future ("in forty years' time"). The first prophecies coincided with the apparition of St. Vincent's heart in April and with those of Our Lord on June 6. They had to do with the downfall of the Bourbons, and were shortly borne out by events.

As a matter of fact, the Revolution of 1830 broke out on July 27. Guns boomed in Paris, blood flowed, King Charles X was obliged to flee into exile, churches were pillaged, crosses overthrown, and the clergy harassed. Monseigneur de Quélen, the archbishop, and a number of other prelates had to disguise themselves and go into hiding.

In religious communities there was much concern, for it was foreseen that there might recur those bloody perse-

4 Elizabeth Ann Bayley, born in New York in 1774, was a member of the Anglican Church. In 1794 she married William Seton, but he died in 1803 during a visit which they were making to Italy. A noted Italian Catholic family, the Filicchis, were very influential in the religious development of Elizabeth Seton. After her return to New York in June 1804, she abjured Protestantism formally (February 27, 1805). She had suffered serious financial reverses and, inasmuch as five children depended on her, she had planned to gain a livelihood by teaching when she came into contact with the French Sulpicians of Baltimore. They persuaded her to settle nearby, and it was at their suggestion and under their direction that she founded, in 1809, the congregation of the Sisters of St. Joseph and established it at Emmitsburg, fifty miles west of Baltimore. They adopted the Rule of St. Vincent de Paul, and Mrs. Seton became their Superior. She died a holy death at Emmitsburg on January 4, 1821.

Thirty years later a group of her religious became united with the Sisters of the Rue du Bac, and are known as Daughters of Charity. Others of them remained independent, and formed a purely American congregation under the name of the Sisters of Charity.

The Daughters of Charity today number about 2,200 members in the United States; the Sisters of Charity about 6,000.

cutions which had been a feature of the Terror and were still remembered vividly. Nevertheless, in conformity with Our Lady's promise, the children of St. Vincent did not suffer during the disturbances. The great annual retreat of the Daughters of Charity was in progress, and continued without molestation. It is true that at first things took a bad turn for the Lazarists; but everything came out in the best way possible.

It was believed among a group called "the Heroes of July" that arms were hidden in the motherhouse in the Rue de Sèvres, and a band of fanatics came to search the place. At their head was a young blackguard who himself made a greater disturbance than did all of his companions together. Not being able to quiet him, the superior said:

"Very well, I will show you our arms."

"Ah, ha; I knew very well that you had them."

"Here they are," and he held out his breviary.

" — !"

"And do you want to see the sort of shot we use in our guns? Look here. . . ." Opening his breviary, the priest displayed the cards of the saints that served him as placemarks while he was reciting his Office.

"Oh! holy pictures! Holy pictures, M. le Curé," cried out the bold ringleader, who was superstitious.

"Do you want one?" asked the priest.

"Ah, yes, if you please, M. le Curé. It will bring me good luck."

The priest gave him a picture and the man was so well satisfied that he went off, thanking the superior and drawing all his companions after him.

Some more of these "heroes" returned on the following days. They were come, they said, to cast down the cross which surmounted the chapel. This time it was M. Étienne (then serving as procurator general) who succeeded in getting rid of them, and the cross was left in its place.

As far as the prophecy referring to a more distant time is concerned, that dealt with the revolution that took place in Paris on the conclusion of the Franco-Prussian war of 1870. We shall see, when the time comes, that all took place just as Our Lady had indicated it would.

3

❧

Revelation of the Miraculous Medal
(1830–1831)

IN THE PRESENCE of Catherine's guardian angel, Our Lady had told her: "God wishes to entrust to you a mission." This mission was made known to her on Saturday, November 27, 1830, the eve of the first Sunday of Advent.

We are again in the chapel of the Rue de Bac where, since five-thirty in the evening, the novices have been gathered for prayer. The silence is complete, and all are absorbed in their devotions. All at once, in the half light, Catherine, who has been kneeling at her place on the Epistle side, hears the rustling of a silken robe, coming from the sanctuary at the right. She trembles, for she recognizes the silky sound that she had marked on the night of July 19. She raises her head.

Once again she has seen the Blessed Virgin. But this time Our Lady stands as if suspended in the air at the right side of the altar, facing Catherine.

"She was of middle height," wrote Catherine, "and she wore a silk robe white as the glow of dawn, of the kind called 'à la Vierge' (a robe fitting close to the neck, and following the lines of the shoulders and arms). A long veil was on her head, and extended to her feet, covering her all over. Through this veil I was able to see her hair in braids held by a piece of lace about an inch wide. Her face was uncovered; but it is so beautiful that I could not describe it."

This is the place in which we must take note of two phases in this most important apparition. In the first Mary offers the world to God; in the second she offers the grace of God to the world.

In the first phase, she bears the aspect which is traditional in representations of the Immaculate Conception. "Her eyes were turned toward heaven, she stood erect upon a large white sphere, her feet were set upon a serpent, greenish in color but touched with yellow spots. At the level of her breast she held a little golden ball surmounted by a Cross, and this she was offering to God."

Both the golden orb and the white sphere represented earth and its peoples. We may remark that although Catherine saw no more than half of the white sphere, she was happy as a patriot to behold on it the shape and name of France.

Suddenly the golden orb was gone; and Our Lady extended her empty hands toward the earth. "On each of her fingers were three precious stones of differing size and from them came rays of light which fell upon the sphere at her feet. But from some of these stones no rays at all were cast.

"Just as I was thinking of this," continues Catherine, "the Blessed Virgin turned her eyes to me, and a Voice spoke within me: 'The sphere which you see is the world; it includes France and every inhabitant of the earth. The rays of light which come from my hands are the graces which I shower on those who ask for them.'

"Our Lady gave me to understand with what generosity and great joy she dispensed grace. 'But,' she said, 'there are graces for which I am not asked, and it is for this reason that some of the stones you see are not sending forth any rays of light.' "

Catherine was now in ecstasy: "I might have been . . . or I might not have been . . . ," she writes in her embarrassed way. "I was full of joy. . . ."

Immediately there began the second phase of the apparition.

A change took place in what Catherine saw before her.

"An oval frame seemed to form, and in its upper portion the following words were inscribed in semicircular form about the upper part of Our Lady's body: O MARY CONCEIVED WITHOUT SIN, PRAY FOR US WHO HAVE RECOURSE TO THEE.

"Once again the Voice made itself heard within my heart: 'Have a medal made after this pattern. Those who wear it, blessed, about their necks and who confidently say this prayer, will receive great graces and will enjoy the special protection of the Mother of God.'

"Then the frame reversed itself to show me the other side of the medal."

What Catherine now saw was Mary's monogram: "A large M, surmounted by a cross having a double bar under it. Beneath this M, the holy hearts of Jesus and Mary were placed side by side, the first being crowned with thorns, the other pierced by a sword. And round about were set twelve stars."

This was the end of the vision.

As will be seen, the mission given to Catherine was a triple one: she was to have the medal struck, she was to spread its use, and she was to promise great favors to those who wore it in a spirit of devotion. To this mission she consecrated the last forty-six years of her life, and she did so in self-effacement of the most absolute kind, and what is even more astonishing, in complete anonymity.

Our Lady returned to Catherine several times to confirm this mission, notably in December of 1830 and in March and in September of 1831. At one time she showed herself during evening prayer, beneath the picture of St. Joseph; at another, above the tabernacle during Mass.

Finally in September 1831, she came for the last time: "After this, my child," she said, "you shall see me no more; but you shall hear my Voice in prayer." This Voice made itself heard whenever Catherine had need of light or of encouragement.

The Voice had already spoken to her, as a matter of fact. While Catherine was grieving because her director would not take her seriously and while she complained: "You can see well enough, dear Mother, that he does not believe me," the Voice had said: "Do not be disturbed! When the time comes, he will do as I wish, for he is my servant, and he would not wish to displease me."

Actually, M. Aladel was showing himself to be quite skeptical. And, in the apparition of September 1831, Our Lady complained that nothing had been done. However, we will allow the confessor to speak for himself on this subject.

In writing to the Abbé Le Guillou, of whom we shall have something to say later, M. Aladel tells how it had taken a year to make him yield:

"From the day following her (first) vision," he wrote, "this novice tried to draw me into the matter; but I saw in it nothing but the work of her imagination, and I strove to convince her of this. As a matter of fact, she went away quietly. When the vision recurred, she came again to tell me of it. I attached no more importance to it this time, and I dismissed her as before. But then, months later, the vision appeared once again and the same things were shown and told to her. The Voice added, this time, that the Blessed Virgin was not pleased with him who had failed to have the medal struck.

"This time, fearing the displeasure of her whom the Church calls the Refuge of Sinners, I could not avoid attaching some significance to the words of the Sister, although I did not let her know this. Then, still in the grip of the notion that all could be no more than an illusion, I failed to do anything about it. However, a few weeks later, it chanced that I had occasion to see the archbishop, and I spoke to him of the matter."

At this time the archbishop of Paris was Monseigneur Louis-Hyacinth de Quélen (1778–1839). This prelate declared to the Lazarist that he found in the account of the apparition "nothing at variance with the faith of the Church and the devotion of the faithful; that, so far as he was concerned, he saw no objection to having such a medal struck"; and that "he wished himself to be the first to be given such a medal."

The archbishop's words spurred M. Aladel on, and he resolved to go forward. But he delayed a few months longer because there was an epidemic of the cholera in Paris and he was occupied in ministering to the victims. It was, therefore, not until May 1832 that he had the medal made. Toward the end of that month, he ordered the engraver, Vachette, to strike fifteen hundred of them, and these were placed at his disposal on June 30.

When Catherine was given her medal, she found that it conformed to the model which had been shown to her, and she said: "I will wear it with veneration; but the important thing now is to make it widely known."

It was the Lazarists and, above all, the Daughters of
Charity, working amidst their pupils and the sick, who set
themselves at once to spread the medal abroad. The
medal did not need to be recommended, for it became
popular almost automatically, and so quickly that the engraver Vachette was overwhelmed with orders.

At the time of the inquiry which was held shortly afterward, he stated that between June 1832 and February
1836 he had manufactured 103,523 medals; but that since
these did not suffice to fill outstanding orders, he had enlisted the aid of other Parisian engravers. The Mint had
supplied him with 420,335, and his colleague, Leclerc,
had furnished 1,223,380. He had also secured 300,000
from some engravers at Lyon.

Yet this was not all; competition entered the picture.
According to Vachette: "There were no more than eleven
engravers in Paris who were able to produce the medals
in large quantities. These were Leplat, Offray, Gache,
Vincent, Collier, Closson, Tresson, Goyon, Bret, Blein
and Dussault."

He had even had lively discussions with some of these
individuals; however, because his own production was in-
adequate, and in deference to the principle that everyone
has a right to make a living when the occasion offers,
he had not thought it necessary to do anything further.

"And how many medals were made by your competi-
tors?" asked the investigator.

"I cannot be sure," said Vachette; "but I am sure that
each of them, in order to recoup his outlay and in order
to obtain some profit, must have put up 200,000 for sale.
I may add that no doubt they sold even more, for I have
it from their lips that they were well satisfied and convinced that this is a good business. For this reason I be-

lieve that in taking this figure of 200,000 as a basis, it is no exaggeration to say that the entire number of medals sold must have been 2,200,000."

After discussing the Parisian market, Vachette went on to speak of other parts of France where the medals were made and sold. He knew very well that at Lyon four manufacturers (of whom three, Changeur, Monterde and Margerie, were known personally to him) had each employed thirty workmen making the medals since 1833. They struck an enormous number, and if we are simply to suppose that they did not exceed his own production, then we may say that from the town of Lyon alone six million medals were put into circulation.

Moreover, Toulouse, Marseilles, Vannes and Bordeaux were occupied as well in the making of the medals. In less than four years, more than eleven million were struck in France. They were also made abroad, particularly in Brussels, Liége, Courtrai, Geneva, Torino, Modena, Bologna, Rome, Naples and London.

At the inquiry, the investigator here asked Vachette: "How many were made abroad?"

Vachette replied: "I do not know. All that I do know is that at Naples the Mint could not cope with the demand, and they ordered 10,000 medals from me, which I sent them."

"And has your own sale of these medals continued?"

"I still sell at least 3,000 a day."

At the very beginning the medal was called "the Medal of the Immaculate Conception," "Mary's Medal," "the Medal of the Daughters of Charity," "the Medal that cures," and so forth. Within two years devout people were calling it "the Miraculous Medal," and this title persisted.

We find this name in the title of a little booklet published by Abbé Le Guillou in 1834 as *Notice historique sur l'origine et les effets de la nouvelle médaille, frappé en l'honneur de l'Immaculée Conception et généralement connue sous le nom de médaille miraculeuse.*

In addition to an account of the apparitions of Our Lady and the letter of M. Aladel which has been cited earlier, this booklet contained particulars of "a number of remarkable occurrences due to the medal in Paris and in the provinces."

However, the Abbé Le Guillou soon gave his booklet into the hands of M. Aladel, and it was the latter who published the *Notice historique* from September 1834 on. In that month 10,000 copies were printed; in December the number increased to 37,600; and so it went. In less than a year 102,304 copies had been circulated. Like Abbé Le Guillou, M. Aladel gave an account of the cures and conversions which had taken place in the case of those who wore the Miraculous Medal.

As an example of M. Aladel's way of setting forth these incidents, here is a passage taken from the third edition (*Notice historique*, December 1834):

"As soon as the medal had been made, it began to become known, especially among the Daughters of Charity. In one of their houses at Paris, they gave medals to all the young girls who were their students. . . . Cholera had broken out again in the city and the sister of one of these students contracted it: all the symptoms were present, diarrhoea, cramps, and vomiting, and there was no question of the seriousness of the illness. The superior had such great trust in the medal that when she was told of the young girl's condition she said: 'Does she not have a medal?' One was immediately given the girl, and she accepted it devoutly. A few minutes afterward, she was completely cured.

"At about the same time, we heard from Meaux that the medal had cured a pregnant woman who had been suffering so seriously from the cholera that the case had been considered hopeless. A few days later she was delivered of a child, and both are now in good health.

"From the same place we learn also of the cure of a child of five who had never been able to walk. It was only after she had consulted the most distinguished physicians and had exhausted all human means, that the distracted mother had recourse to the Blessed Virgin. The medal was placed upon the child, a novena was begun, and on the very first day he was entirely cured of his infirmity. Nor has it recurred."

The *Notice* goes on to say that thanks to the medal "the Daughters of Charity have won to the practice of religion sick people who had refused the sacraments"; that thanks to the medal "many unexpected conversions have taken place."

In the issue of September 1834 about 80 cases of this sort were cited; the following issue reported 130; in the fifth issue there were accounts of 150; by the seventh issue the number had risen to 220, and it went on increasing in the following issues.

It seemed that nothing was able to resist the power of the Miraculous Medal. Monsieur Aladel's little booklet tells us how by contact with the medal cures were effected from "insanity, leprosy, scurvy, tuberculosis, tumors, dropsy, epilepsy, hernia, paralysis, typhoid and other fevers, canker, fractures, scrofula, palpitation of the heart and cholera."

In the spiritual order the medal was responsible for

"the conversion of hardened sinners, of Protestants, of Jews, of apostates, of unbelievers, of Freemasons, of evildoers and of persons of light character." To it were also ascribed wonders "of protection and preservation in war, in shipwreck, in accidents, and in duels."

In respect to duels, the case of Henri Rochefort (1830–1913) is outstanding. This viperish journalist was editor of *La Lanterne,* and he had helped to bring about the fall of the third Napoleon. He was sometimes mixed up in unsavory matters which he had to settle on "the field of honor." On one occasion he ran afoul of Paul de Cassagnac (1840–1904), another well-known journalist who was editor of *Autorité.*

Speaking before a group of Parisians, De Cassagnac's son remarked: "If I may, I should like to tell you the story of a duel which I know especially well: it concerns an encounter between Rochefort and my father.

"They fought over Marie Antoinette. Yes, ladies and gentlemen, so it was; for among the twenty duels which my father fought there was one in defense of the Blessed Virgin, another for Jeanne d'Arc and one in defense of Marie Antionette. As you see, he chose his ladies carefully when he became a knight errant.

"Now Rochefort had published an article most insulting to the memory of Marie Antoinette. My father replied even more sharply, and Rochefort sent his seconds to arrange a duel. Inasmuch as at the time the laws which forbade dueling were being strictly enforced, they decided to fight in Belgium. However, all became known, the Belgian police were advised of the project, and when the principals and their seconds reached the frontier they were turned back. They took the train to Paris, and got off at the Gare du Nord, determined to put an end to the matter at once. They hired a carriage and drove toward the northern outskirts of the city. When they had passed the fortifications at Briche, they stopped and took their positions. It was midwinter, the weather was very cold, and snow covered the ground. The pistol was the weapon they had chosen, and conditions were particularly trying, for their silhouettes stood out boldly against the whiteness of the snow.

"According to usage, Charles de Puyferrat, chief second to Rochefort, gave my father his gun. 'I will fire from the waist,' said my father. When the word was given he held his pistol aloft. Rochefort drew and missed. My father lowered his arm, pressed the trigger, and Rochefort rolled over in the snow. They thought he was dead, but it was not so. The bullet had struck the Miraculous Medal of silver which a woman friend of Rochefort had sewed to his clothing the evening before. The contact had blunted the bullet which was thus turned from its course and made no more than a bloody scratch.

"On the following day, Louis Veuillot (1813–1883), in a well-known article, recalled that Rochefort, when he was young, had written a sonnet in honor of the Immaculate Conception, and that he had received a prize for it at Toulouse. 'M. Rochefort,' wrote Veuillot, 'the Virgin owed you this; but do not presume upon it again, for she has paid her debt, and henceforth you are quits.'

"After my father's death, Rochefort told this story to my brother and myself, and with his characteristically boyish smile he added: 'Yes, my dear friends, that was how it happened. This medal was of silver, and I must say that it is the only time in my life that I have had silver where it was needed.' "

In the very beginning of its history, a great triumph for the Miraculous Medal took place in the case of an old prelate whose conduct had been a cause of much scandal to the Church. This was Baron Dominique de Riom de Frolhiac de Fourt de Pradt (1759–1837), who was known as the Abbé de Pradt.

His life had not been an edifying one, for he had been chiefly occupied in a search for honors and fortune, and his attitude toward the Holy See was wanting in respect. Napoleon I had showered him with favors and had named him bishop of Poitiers. Later, in order to reward him for his diplomatic services, the emperor gave him the archbishopric of Malines in Belgium. This nomination was made against the wishes of the Pope with which the prelate did not much concern himself.

De Pradt ungratefully contributed to the downfall of Napoleon, and made friends with the Bourbons by aiding in their restoration to the throne of France. King Louis XVIII showed his liking for De Pradt by loading him with honors and distinctions and also by conferring a large pension upon him. He was the recipient of another pension from the Belgian government as the price of his renunciation of the See of Malines, and of a third from Bolivar whom he had aided in his revolt against Spain.

The Abbé had been devoting his later years to improving agricultural conditions in Auvergne, and in producing a variety of writings which were giving joy to the enemies of the Church. Now that he seemed about ready to die, his irreligious friends were occupied with plans for the splendid anticlerical funeral ceremonies they hoped to hold, for no one even suspected that he would die other than impenitently.

He had refused, as a matter of fact, even to hear mention made of a return to religion, and on several occasions he had denied Monseigneur de Quélen access to his house. However, the archbishop decided to make one final attempt. Wearing the Miraculous Medal, Monseigneur de Quélen went once again to see the dying De Pradt. The servants and nurses, all of whom knew of the orders which had previously been given by their master, refused to admit the archbishop, and he went sadly away.

He had no more than reached home when a messenger rushed in to apologize on behalf of the Abbé de Pradt: he was desolated at what had happened; his people had been acting on outdated orders, he begged that the archbishop would honor him with a visit. Monseigneur de Quélen hastened to comply with this request.

It seems that when the hardened old sinner had learned of the prelate's first visit, he was so touched that his sentiments had changed instantaneously. He welcomed the archbishop and begged forgiveness for the trouble he had caused him, confessed his sins and deplored the scandal he had given. He received the last Sacraments from the archbishop, and died in his arms on the following night.

Monseigneur de Quélen himself told of this conversion, and he attributed it to the Miraculous Medal.

4

✤

Parisian Inquiry and Roman Approbation

CATHERINE left the motherhouse at the conclusion of her eight months' stay in the seminary, and on February 5, 1831, was assigned to the Hospice d'Enghien in the Rue de Picpus. This was located in the section of Paris known as Reuilly, about two miles from the Rue du Bac.

This little resthome, founded in memory of the Duc d'Enghien,[1] then served as a shelter for about fifty elderly men and women. The seven religious who attended them did not form an independent community: they were subject to the superiors of the Maison d'Oeuvres, a more important establishment located in the Rue de Reuilly. The two houses were separated only by a garden, and the Sisters at the Hospice d'Enghien could easily pass over to attend the conventual exercises which were held in the Maison d'Oeuvres.

Ma Sœur Labouré, as Catherine was called, was for some years cook and seamstress at the Hospice. After 1836 she was given special charge of the male patients. She was also responsible for the poultry-yard and served as portress as well.

For almost forty years, then, her chief work consisted in waiting upon and taking care of about thirty old men,

[1] The Duc d'Enghien (1772–1804), son of the Prince de Condé, was accused of conspiring against the Empire. On the orders of Napoleon I, he was seized while on German territory, brought to Paris and shot.

some of whom must have been difficult. She had to see that they ate and slept well, that they were clean and properly dressed for the changing seasons and that they were nursed and coddled a bit when ill, that they had tobacco in their pouches, and on days when they went out a few pennies in their purses besides. All this was Catherine's concern. She had also to keep them occupied, to make them feel that they were not alone in the world, and that they were loved. She had to scold them, to compose their quarrels, to persuade them to say their prayers, and, when the time came, to see that they received the last rites.

Catherine had to be everything to these old men, and to fashion her role on that of a mother who avoids being either too indulgent or too severe. When she left them it was not for long, and then only that she might go to the Rue de Bac.

What must have been her joy to retrace her steps in the corridor where she had walked side by side with her guardian angel; to return to pray in the chapel where she had been granted such great favors.

It was during these visits to the motherhouse that she had her last two visions: one was in March 1831; and the second, at which Our Lady expressed her dissatisfaction because of the delay in the production of the medal, was in September 1831.

It would seem that no religious led a life more ordinary, more monotonous than Catherine. She worked, she did as she was told, she prayed, and she kept silent.

One realizes that she had little time for letter writing. There is but one letter that is worth mentioning. It is addressed to Marie-Louise when in 1834 the older sister had decided to abandon her vocation after having spent sixteen years in the convent.

We last saw Marie-Louise as superior at Castelsarrasin. Why did she suddenly withdraw from the community? Was she ill? Had she had difficulties with the higher superiors? Had her fervor entirely cooled? She was convinced that her way of life had become unbearable, and, as is always the case, she was able to give the best of reasons for abandoning it.

"God himself," she said, "has miraculously made this known to me."

Catherine, however, thought this notion to be wholly illusory, and she wrote to her sister: "Before you return to our childhood home, I am sending you a letter which ought to give you some pleasure. It is the letter you wrote me when I first thought of entering the community."

This was the letter — some few lines of which we have cited already — which had been received by Catherine at the time she was serving in the bistro of Charles Labouré. Marie-Louise, who wrote fluently, had thus praised the congregation to which she wished to attract her sister:

"To be a Daughter of Charity," she had written, "is to give oneself to God wholeheartedly in order to serve Him in his poor, to console the unfortunate, to be compassionate to the unhappy, solacing them in their woes, and helping them to die in the love of God.

"How noble is this work! It is to follow in the steps of Jesus. It is to be angels of His loving kindness, dispensers of His goodness, means through which His help is given to men. It is to be clothed with the most lovable of His own attributes.

"The state of a (contemplative) religious has the appearance of being in some ways more perfect (than is ours). We are not required, as they are, to practice austerities, to make use of hair shirts or the discipline. Yet in the place of these things we put our very way of life, a way of life which seems to the world very difficult, for the world knows not our inward consolations.

"These consolations are such that, if I were to be offered in exchange for them not merely a kingdom but even the whole world, I would regard such a suggestion as the dust under my feet, for I am persuaded that I should not find even in possessing the whole world the happiness and contentment which has been mine in my vocation.

"Think whether it be not a better thing to serve God than the world in the short space of time which we have to spend on this earth. Therefore, if God is calling you, go to Him; for from every point of view, He is the most worthy object you can seek."

It was this letter that Catherine now set before Marie-Louise.

"What you then urged me to do," she went on to say, "do you now do yourself; it is time that you put into practice the good advice which you then gave me. Say again to yourself all that you said to me, that you may know that you will never find, even if you gain the whole earth, the happiness you have known in your religious calling.

"And would you give up this happiness for a trifle? In the face of a temptation? We are indeed weak when we do not place all our confidence in God.

"I must say that it has pained me very much to note that almost all your letters speak of miracles, as though God wrought them for light causes. We are indeed weak creatures when we hope that He will work miracles for our convenience. You speak of one having taken place

when you left the community. Alas! God knows if this
be a miracle! . . . Did Our Lord, the Blessed Virgin, or
the saints have much to say about their miracles? What is
become of your sense of humility? It is far from being like
theirs. We might even say that you lack it entirely.

"Farewell! I urge you to go back to our parents' home;
there you will be alone, and God will speak to your heart.
Think upon our Mother's death. You were with her at
that time. Think upon our Father's death, which has happened but lately. Thought of death is the best means of
regaining God's grace."

Catherine's letter is full of charity and good sense. Yet,
we must confess, nevertheless, that it is sharp and its irony
even rather cruel. It may indicate that Catherine was not
wholly familiar with the Gospel, else she would have
known that Our Lord constantly spoke of His miracles
as proofs of His mission.

Whatever the case, the letter was well received, and no
doubt the tone of it must have been fitting enough, for the
desired end was achieved. We must remember, too, that
she who had seen Mary would have poured out her prayers to her that her sister might be drawn to do God's will.

Marie-Louise did ask and obtain forgiveness for her
withdrawal, and once again took her place among the
Daughters of Charity. She became ill — or relapsed again
into illness — and before she died, she spent many a year
in the infirmary at the motherhouse. Catherine often came
to visit her; but it was she who survived not only Catherine but Tonine as well.

With the spread of the Miraculous Medal the responsibility of the religious authorities increased. How scandal-
ous would it have been in the eyes of believers, what an
excuse for mocking reports in the anti-clerical press, were

it to appear one day that the new devotion had its roots in the fancies of a novice who might be an impostor.

St. Vincent de Paul's congregations were especially anxious to be above reproach in the affair, and on February 11, 1836, M. Aladel and M. Étienne, the procurator general of the Lazarists, asked the diocesan authorities to conduct an official inquiry. On the day following Monseigneur de Quélen so ordered.

There are some courts of inquiry which, however well or ill conducted they may be, arrive finally at a result known in advance. This court was impartial and searching. It was conducted by Canon Quentin, vicar general and *promoter fidei* of the diocese of Paris. He was a man who knew his business and who carried it out both conscientiously and efficiently. He took much trouble to verify the testimony personally: it was for this reason that he wished to examine the books of the engraver Vachette, in order to determine exactly how many medals had been circulated.

He cited forty-eight witnesses. All were respectable individuals who offered their testimony under oath and were given full opportunity to speak freely. Among the witnesses we find M. Aladel and M. Étienne. Among them, however, as we shall see, we do not find Catherine.

Nineteen sessions were held between February 16 and July 13, 1836.

The following two passages, taken from the report of the inquiry, may serve as specimens of the interrogations and replies made and received. Canon Quentin questioned M. Aladel as follows:

Quentin: At the time of the vision how old was the Sister?

Aladel: About twenty-four years of age.

Quentin: What is her social origin in the world?

Aladel: She comes of a family of the peasantry.

Quentin: How well educated is she?

Aladel: Only to the most ordinary extent.

Quentin: How long had she been at the seminary before having the vision?

Aladel: About six months.

Quentin: Is there anything unusual about her devotional life?

Aladel: It was then, as it is now, of the most simple and proper sort.

Quentin: Does she have special devotion to Our Lady?

Aladel: There is nothing external in its manifestation in the sense that would make it appear remarkable, but it is evident that she feels great confidence in the Blessed Virgin.

Quentin: Is this woman truthful and honest?

Aladel: She is quite truthful, and there is nothing unusual in her behavior.

Quentin: Is there ground for believing that her imaginative faculty may be fanatical?

Aladel: On the contrary, her manner is rather cold; she seems almost apathetic.

The hearing of February 19 was devoted to the interrogation of M. Étienne who had been in the confidence of Catherine's confessor (M. Aladel) from the very beginning.

Quentin: What sort of opinion of the character and imaginative faculties of this Sister have you received from M. Aladel?

Étienne: M. Aladel has spoken to me of a very devout and honest woman, characterized by complete purity of life and entirely lacking in imaginative fanaticism, being rather quiet in temperament.

Quentin: Has this Sister been so careful to preserve the secret of her vision that neither the superior general nor the other Sisters have learned of it from her?

Étienne: She has been wholly silent about all that has happened. This silence ought to be all the more highly esteemed in view of the little attention that M. Aladel paid to her story, and because of his repeated refusals to agree to her entreaties for his attention to it. That he had not seemed to take her seriously might indeed have been thought by her a sufficient reason for discussing the matter either with her superiors or with someone else; but she did not do so.

Quentin: Are you aware of the motives which underlie the determination of this Sister to remain unknown even now that the medal has been made?

Étienne: I join M. Aladel in believing that these motives are to be found in her deep humility which has led her to avoid in this manner the attention which might center upon her.

Having completed his interrogation and interviewing of witnesses, and having verified the testimony, Canon Quentin presented a report of about ten thousand words to Monseigneur de Quélen.

As had been the case with the inquiry, the object of the report was twofold: it was concerned with the reality of the apparitions as well as with the reality of the prodigies attributed to the medal.

As far as concerned the first of these, the question was to learn if Our Lady had really appeared and asked that the medal be struck. In other words, was Catherine possibly a deceitful liar or a self-deceived fanatic?

The substance of M. Aladel's reply was that she was not a liar; he had been her confessor for six years, during which time he had observed her without partiality, and he had never known her to lie. He had found in her perfect rectitude and truthfulness, her solid piety being of such sort as to make her incapable of trickery.

Nor was she, on the other hand, a creature of illusions. She was in no sense an actress, fascinated with some chosen role and ending by taking it seriously; nor was she the hysterical slave of a nervous disorder; nor yet was she a fanatic at the mercy of an over-excited imagination which would invent incidents and then embrace them as being realities.

Her conduct displayed neither singularities not extravagance. She was a self-contained peasant girl of good common sense, unimpressed by the unusual and unattracted by what is out of the ordinary. She was not a reader, nor did she fancy herself in any special role; she sought only to walk the common path with her Sisters, and to be left in peace.

Moreover, she was "too limited in imagination to have conjured up the picture she had painted, or to have put together the parts of the inscription in such a way as would have been appropriate as a pattern for a medal." Such is my penitent, he seems to say, and this is what she has ever been.

It was the humility of the Sister that broke down the

resistance of M. Aladel and that won the support of M. Étienne. Are not humble souls generally sincere? Are they not naturally armed against those appearances that would throw them into the limelight?

Canon Quentin was not less impressed than they by the remarkable humility of the young Sister. Her own conduct was her best recommendation, he observed, both as she was before and as she remained after the medal had begun to become known.

It was, it seemed to him, remarkable that she had for so long ceased to speak of her vision to M. Aladel even though it was repeated. If she finally returned to the subject, it was to settle her unrest, to recover her peace of soul, and because the Blessed Virgin had expressed her own disappointment. Could it be said that her reluctance to speak rested in the certainty that she would again be treated as a dreamer? Yet her troubled state of mind was not considered by her as a reason for speaking to others, to her superiors, for example, of the apparition and of the command to have a medal fashioned to represent it. She remained silent; she kept her secret. Thus she sought for nothing but obscurity and silence.

The report records an incident which took place at the Maison d'Oeuvres at Reuilly at the beginning of 1832. The report of the apparition having gone around, the Sisters of the two communities at Reuilly and Enghien were plying their confessor, M. Aladel, with questions. Catherine was in their midst. "How could I," asks M. Aladel, "how could I reply unrestrainedly and yet not betray her? Placing myself in the hands of Mary, I told the story of the wonderful vision, and I was struck with admiration of the good Sister whom I had feared to disturb and upset; for she kept her natural manner, she mingled in the general interchange of comment in the same open way as did the others. She gave no evidence in either attitude or appearance that she was not considering something which had happened to someone else."

The report goes on to state that after four years her desire to remain hidden was unchanged; even though the medal had now become celebrated, no one even knew Catherine's name. And was not the best proof of her humility found in her refusal to meet the bishop, a refusal which had resulted in the inquiry being conducted without her presence at it.

In the preceding year M. Aladel had exerted every effort to persuade Catherine to speak to Monseigneur de Quélen who wished to see her. She refused even to the extent of being unwilling to discuss the matter with him from behind a curtain.

At the time of the inquiry he had abstained from renewing his attempt to bring her forth. He knew that the effort would be vain, and he indicated, in addition, that the appearance of the Sister would be useless because she now seemed to remember almost nothing of what had occurred.

It will be said that this is a strange loss of memory. Yet it was not the first, nor was it to be the last, of such lapses.

In the course of the year before, when the painter Lecerf was working on the picture of the apparition that M. Aladel had ordered from him, this artist wished to know what had been the color of the Virgin's veil. M. Aladel did not recall. He wrote to Catherine and asked her in general terms to tell him again how the Blessed Virgin had looked. "It is impossible for me to recall now all that I have seen," was her reply. "The only detail which is fixed in my recollection is that Our Lady's veil was of gleaming white."

This time, she knew only what she needed to know. At another time, she knew nothing at all. Years later, M. Aladel being dead, it was M. Étienne who, believing he had pierced the identity of the seer, sought to have her tell of the apparition. His attempt was as fruitless as had been any of the others, even though at the time he was superior general of both congregations. Brought before him, Catherine, who had been told by Our Lady to speak of the vision to her confessor alone, said that she no longer recalled what had taken place during that period in her life.

Were these losses of memory natural things, or were they the result of divine intervention? . . . So far as 1836 is concerned, Canon Quentin refrained from coming to a decision. He did not invoke the juridical means which were at his disposal in order to compel the appearance of the Sister at the inquiry he was conducting.

"According to the regular process of an inquiry," he wrote, "it is from the lips of the young Sister herself that ecclesiastical authority ought to hear the details of the vision; it is by her that information concerning the circumstances of the apparition should be given; and it would be by her sworn testimony that the accuracy and truth of her tale would be given assurance and guarantee. But the *promotor fidei* recognizes that there are reasons — because God has His own way of accomplishing things — which hinder the fulfillment of formalities and conditions ordinarily deemed essential. The promotor has therefore confined himself to establishing the motives for this hindrance which he has found to exist."

As for the two motives involved here — a sudden loss of memory and reluctance to come forward — we may note that as regards the second Catherine believed that she had the right to remain unknown. As a matter of fact, from the time she first told her confessor she had authorized him to speak of her vision; indeed, she had urged him to do so; but at the same time she had exacted of him an express promise that her own name was to be revealed to no one.

Inasmuch as the Sister who had had the vision remained unknown and out of reach, all was then based on the testimony of M. Aladel alone. It is for this reason that the investigator was so concerned to establish that testimony as being above attack.

Canon Quentin describes M. Aladel as "a priest of commendable knowledge and virtue. Now assistant to the superior general, he owes this office to his reputation among his confrères, and their confidence in him is a title to the respect of the diocesan authority to whom, moreover, he is well known.

"In this affair his conduct has been marked by wisdom, prudence and thoughtful care. Despite the repetition of the vision, he himself distrusted it at first, and he did all in his power to convince his penitent of the possibility of self-deceit. It was only after a year and a half that he began to doubt his decision under the fear of being a cause of disappointment to the Virgin. He then went to lay before the feet of your Lordship the disturbance within his soul, and to seek your paternal advice."

As to the suggestion that M. Aladel might have himself "invented the story of the vision and could not bring forward the Sister for investigation for the reason that he did not know such a Sister," this suggestion Quentin regarded as "a calumny so odious" as not to merit refutation.

The fact is that M. Aladel was honesty itself. Those who knew him in life, or scrutinized his life after his death, discovered nothing that offers ground for suspicion: all is open, worthy and wise; he was a man who had walked always in God's sight and according to the Gospel. His whole life was such that he justly merits being called exemplary.[2]

The second subject of the inquiry was, we are told, the reality of the spiritual and temporal "prodigies" ascribed to the medal.

Of the hundreds of cures attributed to it six were examined and declared to be without natural explanation; of the conversions produced by the medal, three were examined and judged equally mysterious and impressive.

But of themselves would not the figures for the sale of the medals, figures which continued to increase progressively as the report was being written, would not these be enough to indicate some heavenly concern in the whole matter? Canon Quentin thought the answer to this question should be "Yes."

The conclusion reached in his report to the archbishop was that there was no evidence of "anything fantastic" in the affair; that on the contrary the events "seem real and worthy of credence." Nevertheless, the inquiry did not terminate in the official canonical declaration that had been awaited. Why Monseigneur de Quélen did not formally

[2] All this is set forth in the work entitled *Vie, vertus et mort de M. Aladel.* Cf. Lucien Misermont, C.M.: *La bienheureuse Catherine Labouré et la Médaille miraculeuse; documents, aperçu critique* (Paris, 1933), p. 197.

declare himself is not known. Did he perhaps expect that the identity of the Sister might be revealed? Or did he feel that from Rome there would soon come approval of a sort that would be effective throughout the Christian world?

During the remaining three years of his life, Monseigneur de Quélen did not cease to give evidence of his belief in the authenticity of the apparition which had taken place in the Rue de Bac. And he spoke with increasing frequency of the Miraculous Medal.

On December 15, 1836, in announcing to the people of his charge the forthcoming dedication of the Church of Notre Dame de Lorette, he said in his pastoral letter: "It is true that graces of healing and of salvation seem to multiply according to our fervor in imploring Mary's tender mercy. Therefore we urge the faithful to wear the medal struck in recent years and to repeat frequently the prayer inscribed upon it: 'O Mary conceived without sin, pray for us who have recourse to thee.' "

In 1837 he allowed a painting of what Catherine had seen to be placed in the Church of Saint-Germain. In 1838 he besought Pope Gregory XVI to add to Our Lady's litany the prayer which she had herself revealed to Catherine Labouré: *Regina sine labe concepta, ora pro nobis*: "O Mary conceived without sin, pray for us." When this request was granted, he made joyful announcement of it in a new pastoral letter to the Catholics of Paris.

Finally, in 1839, but a few weeks before he died, he caused to be installed at Notre Dame a large bronze statue, made after the manner of the figure on the medal.[3] And

---

[3] Of the churches here referred to Notre Dame de Lorette and Saint-Germain are two of the parish churches of Paris, while Notre-Dame is the cathedral.

this statue was simply a larger version of a little statue he kept beside him, and before which he was accustomed to pray every day.

The name of this devout prelate must always be associated with that of St. Catherine Labouré. Not only did he have sufficient supernatural insight to believe in the truth of the apparition and sufficient courage to profess his belief; it is also due to him that the medal was struck and put into circulation; and it is to him that we owe the inquiry conducted at Paris by his vicar, Canon Quentin, an inquiry whose findings served as the foundation for the approval finally granted by the Roman Curia.

The most important evidence of the stamp of official approval was the institution, in 1894, of a liturgical feast of the Miraculous Medal: *Festum sub titulo Manifestationis Immaculatae Virginis a Sacro Numismate* — the Feast of the Apparition of Our Lady of the Miraculous Medal. The universal Church keeps this feast on November 27, the anniversary of the day on which there took place the chief of the apparitions which have been decribed above.

5

❧

Conversion of Alphonse Ratisbonne
(1842)

LINKED to the very beginnings of the story of the Miraculous Medal is the conversion of Alphonse Ratisbonne (1814–1884). It seems, as a matter of fact, that never before had Our Lady obtained anything more extraordinary from her Son than this conversion. We might add, anything more difficult if we did not know that it is no more difficult for God to call a sun into being than to feed the sparrows.

There existed no reason why Ratisbonne should have become a Catholic; on the contrary, there seemed to be every reason against his conversion. Ordinarily, the soul is disposed to receive the grace of conversion by suffering or unrest, by the thought of death and judgment, by the desire to pray and to believe as does some loved one, or by the trials and disillusionments of life, the need of pardon, of light, of peace, as the case may be. Generally speaking, the grace of conversion is not given to scoffers; especially is this true in respect to those who are intent upon refusing that grace. And generally, too, it takes its own time to mature. After it has been granted, usually there is a period of waiting, in which the converted soul learns certain things. Seldom is the soul precipitately endowed with knowledge of all that it had, hitherto, been unaware of.

In the case of Ratisbonne, every one of the general rules was upset and transversed.

Ratisbonne himself tells us, in a letter written two and a half months afterward, how this chain of events came about.[1] To a large extent we shall give the story in his own words, departing from them only to condense the narration a bit here and there for the sake of clarity.

Atheism and Frivolity

Tobie-Alphonse Ratisbonne, who later adopted the name of Marie-Alphonse Ratisbonne, was born at Strasbourg (Alsace, France) on May 1, 1814. He was the ninth child of a family of bankers who were related or allied to the Rothschilds, the Worms, the Goulds, and other wealthy Jewish families.

"My family," he writes, "is well known as being rich and charitable, and for this reason has long been considered as of the first rank in Alsace. Christians as well as Jews have held in benediction the name of my grandfather; and he was the only Jew who obtained from Louis XVI not merely the right to hold property in Strasbourg, but titles of nobility as well."

This maternal grandfather, thus ennobled at a time when European Jews were treated as pariahs and confined to ghettos, was called Theodore Cerfbeer. He loaned money to princes, and gave it to the needy. Alphonse inherited both his generosity and his kindness of heart. While still a child, he lost both parents, but he was, of

---

[1] This letter, addressed to M. l'Abbé Dufriche-Desgenettes on April 12, 1842, is taken from *Conversion de Marie-Alphonse Ratisbonne*, new ed. (Paris, 1919). Consult also: Th. de Bussières, *L'enfant de Marie* (Paris, 1842); M. Aladel, *Notice*, 8ème. éd. (Paris, 1842), pp. 391–449; *Le T. R. P. Marie-Alphonse Ratisbonne* (Paris, 1903), pp. 206–92; and *Deux maisons de Sion* (Paris, 1935), pp. 25–37.

course, a member of one of those Jewish dynasties
wherein, as in princely families, all regard themselves as
forming a unit so close-knit that no member of the clan
is ever abandoned. "I found in my good uncle, the patri-
arch of our family, a second father; for he had no children
of his own, and he therefore lavished all his affection
upon those of his brother."

Alphonse became his uncle's favorite, which he merited
by a rare combination of gifts: he was of a noble spirit
and endowed with artistic talents; he was imaginative
and possessed an air of distinction, good looks and charm.
He was one of those attractive beings who bring beauty
into the lives of their fellowmen, who put gloom to flight,
and who can have as many friends as they wish.

His family was entirely without any sort of religious
leaning whatsoever: "Neither in the home of my uncle
nor among my brothers and sisters was there the least
attempt to practise Judaism. I was a Jew in name; that
was all. I did not even believe in God."

His intellectual training was equally atheistic. "I began
my studies in the Collège Royal of Strasbourg; and here
I made more progress in the corruption of my heart than
in the development of my mind."

Nevertheless, he was intellectually gifted and success in
his studies came easily and without effort on his own part.
"I was taken out of the Collège Royal to be enrolled in
a Protestant institution where the sons of the great Protestant houses of Alsace and Germany went to prepare
themselves for the fashionable life in Paris, giving themselves over rather to pleasure than to learning. However,
after having sat for the final examinations, I found rather
by good fortune than by merit that I was entitled to the
bachelor's degree." It would appear from his references

to "the corruption of the heart" and "pleasure" that the sixth commandment had become a dead letter to him.

He went to Paris to study law. This was at the very time when the apparitions were taking place in the Rue de Bac; but it was also the golden hour of the anti-clericals in French politics and literature. One has but to think of Michelet, Quinet, Eugène Sue, and Béranger to recall the writings against the Jesuits which were then so popular throughout Europe.

"After gaining my degree in law, and donning the advocate's robe, I was recalled to Strasbourg by my uncle who, indeed, made every effort to attach me to himself. I would be unable to catalogue the gifts he showered upon me: horses, carriages, trips. His generosity overwhelmed me in a thousand ways, and he did not refuse to fulfill my slightest whim.

"To these testimonies of his affection he added a more positive mark of his confidence when he made me a member of his firm and promised me the title and prerogatives of his associate. This promise he actually carried out on January 1, 1842; and I heard of it while I was in Rome."

But we are going too fast; we shall not be concerned with Rome for several years. For the present the scene is laid in Paris where our young dandy goes on his pleasure trips, or in Strasbourg where he devotes himself to charitable works.

"There was but one point upon which my uncle reproached me, and that was the matter of my frequent visits to Paris. 'You are over-fond of the Champs-Elysées,' he said to me in his indulgent fashion. He was right. Although a certain natural shyness caused me to withdraw from ignoble associations, I thought only of my own pleasure, for I imagined that one lives to enjoy life, and I gave myself over to this wholeheartedly."

However, young Ratisbonne had found a way of expressing his natural generosity, and to this he gave some of his time. "Happily, I now became interested in a good work which offered an outlet for my need to be active. This was the *Société d'encouragement au travail des jeunes Israélites* (Society to Encourage the Work of Young Israelites). I became one of the most active of its members, and made large contributions to its treasury." Often enough, he depleted his own funds by his benefactions to the society.

Although he differed from his brother Theodore, whom we are soon to meet, yet in two ways he resembled him, for both men were passionately devoted to their fellow Jews and both were free from the love of money for its own sake.

"I am unaware," said Theodore, "how or whence I acquired the antipathy I have always had for gold and silver, but in this sense I have ever been unlike many Jews."

Alphonse never had a clear notion of the contents of his note case. When he got out of a hired cab, he would give the case to the driver and ask him to help himself to the price of the journey. Then he would return the case to his pocket without even looking to see what amount had been removed.

Betrothal and Anti-Catholicism

"In the midst of all this abundance," Alphonse writes, "there was an emptiness in my heart: something was wanting. But even this lack was to be filled. My niece, the daughter of my eldest brother, had been promised to me as my bride since we were children. She grew in charm under my very eyes, and in her I saw all my hopes of the future, and of the happiness which it held for me."

She is spoken of in contemporary memoirs as being beautiful, intelligent and kind. Flore Ratisbonne was to have her own hour of notoriety. At this period she was as wanting as was Alphonse in any sense of religion.

"It seems to me," writes the young man in the letter which we are citing, "it seems to me that it would not be decorous to embark here upon the praise of my fiancée; but all who were acquainted with her know how difficult it would be to picture a young woman more sweet, more lovable, or more gracious."

One may imagine how much he loved her. He had, indeed, a great capacity for loving. He was so tender of heart and so sensitive in his nature that he was always unable to take leave of his family or friends without weeping. It has been told in the house of mutual friends that whenever he left after a visit he would do so by stealth, going off before dawn in order that he might avoid the sadness of farewells.

Flore "was in my eyes a special being who seemed to have been created that she might be my own completion. When the wishes of our relations, so agreeable to our mutual feelings, finally resulted in the determination that this long-desired marriage would take place, I believed that henceforth nothing could mar my happiness."

The betrothal ceremony was held in August 1841. "I saw all my family filled with joy; my sisters were especially happy! . . . They had but one thing against me, saying that I loved my fiancée so greatly that they were jealous of her. . . . For I ought to have told you that few broth-

ers and sisters loved one another more or were more
united than we. Our love for one another verged on idol-
atry.

"There was only one member of my family who was
not included in this love, for I detested him. This was
my brother Theodore." Fifteen years prior to this time,
Theodore, then a law student, had come under the influence of the Abbé Bautain, an ontologist who was then
highly esteemed among philosophers. The young man's
father had become disturbed by rumors that had reached
him and had summoned him to a discussion.

As Theodore put it: "My father spoke to me in strong
terms. Having recalled all the marks of love and confidence
he had shown me he then asked me point-blank if I were
a Christian.

" 'Yes,' I replied, 'I am, and my Christian faith impels
me to renounce the pleasures of life in order that I may
devote myself to the welfare of my fellow Jews.' "

Alphonse describes this as "a heavy blow to our family,
for they had great hopes in regard to my brother."

Theodore was baptized in December 1827. Three years
afterward, "in spite of all entreaties to the contrary, and
disregarding the sorrow which he had caused us, he went
even further. He became a priest and he began to exercise his ministry at Strasbourg in the very face of our
family, who were grief-stricken.

"Young as I was [Alphonse was then sixteen] I considered his behavior revolting, and I hated him in his
own person and in his profession. Educated as I had been
in the midst of young Christians who were as indifferent
as I myself in religious matters, I had hitherto neither
liking not antipathy for Christianity. However, I considered my brother's conversion an act of madness, and I

ascribed it to the fanaticism of Catholics whom I began to hold in horror. His profession repelled me; his company I found offensive; and as for his grave and serious manner of speech — it drove me to desperation."

As dogmatic and authoritative as Alphonse was impulsive, jaunty and off-handed, Theodore was not entirely easy to get along with. This was true at least of men, for his spiritual daughters held him in adoration. There was to come a time when all but one of the members of the congregation of the Priests of Zion which he had founded were to desert him. After the two brothers became reconciled, they loved each other deeply; but it was said that they never got on so well as when they were separated by some hundreds of miles.

"A year before my betrothal," continues Alphonse's narrative, "I was unable to control my ill will toward him, and I expressed it in a letter designed to break forever any connection between us. When the son of one of our brothers was near death Theodore had dared to ask the child's parents to allow him to baptize the boy and perhaps was already preparing to do it when I heard about it. I wrote that I looked upon his behavior as base and unworthy, that as a priest he ought rather concern himself with men than with infants; and I added so many insults and threats that even today it astonishes me that he did not retort. He continued to see my family; but I did not wish even to look at him, and I cherished a bitter detestation of priests, convents and above all of Jesuits, the mere mention of whom provoked me to fury.

"Fortunately, my brother left Strasbourg. This was what I had hoped for. His going relieved me of a great burden. . . . Nevertheless, I yielded to the persuasion of my relatives at the time of my betrothal, and I wrote him a few words of apology. He replied to me in a friendly fashion, and spoke of the needs of his poor so that I finished by contributing some trifling sum for their benefit. After this I had no further relations with Theodore; I never thought of him; indeed, I had completely forgotten him. . . ."

Flore Ratisbonne being only sixteen at the time of her engagement to Alphonse, and since the marriage was not to take place until a year had elapsed, it was deemed proper for the future couple to be separated during the intervening time. "I was to take a pleasure trip," says Alphonse, "while awaiting the time of our marriage. Yet I did not know in what direction to travel. One of my sisters lived in Paris, and wished me to visit her; a close friend invited me to Valencia in Spain; but I finally hit upon the thought of going direct to Naples, of passing the winter at Malta and of returning home by way of Constantinople."

But before we set out with him upon his journey, let us take some note of the feelings with which he began it.

"I must here describe," he says, "a certain change which had begun to affect my religious ideas at this period. I had never believed in anything, but the sight of my fiancée aroused in me some indescribable feeling of human dignity. I looked upon her as my good angel, and I told her so. The thought of her roused my heart to the thought of a God whom I did not know. I began to believe in the soul's immortality, and I instinctively turned to prayer to thank God for my happiness."

One who is filled to the uttermost limit of his being with love crosses easily the line which divides atheism from deism. How can one fail to hope for eternal existence in the act of ceaselessly reiterating vows of everlasting love?

How can one conceive of the existence of a noble being whom one loves to distraction and with whom one wishes to live forever, unless there be a God? Unhappily, the actual experience of marriage often leaves deists of this sort less convinced and less fervent.

It must be remarked that Alphonse's deism did not in any way diminish his hostility to the idea of a revealed religion and to all churches. He continues his description of his own ideas:

"I should note also that, shortly prior to my leaving Strasbourg, many famous Israelites gathered there in order to discuss ways of reforming Judaism and bringing it into harmony with the thought of the day. I went to their meeting where each one of those present expressed his feelings about the projected improvements.

"There was prolonged discussion: much was said of human custom, of the exactions of the day; of public opinion; of civilization. But one thing was forgotten: the law of God. I do not know that the name of God was even mentioned, nor that of Moses, nor the Bible.

"It was my own opinion that all forms of religion ought to be put aside, that recourse should be neither to (holy) books nor to men (Moses and the Prophets); I thought rather that every man ought to practice his own belief as he understood it."

Alphonse then refers to another of his characteristics. "Before starting on my journey I determined to sign a whole set of acquittances for advances made to the *Société d'encouragement au travail*. I dated them for January 15, 1842. I was so tired out from writing this date that I said to myself, as I cast my pen aside: God knows where I shall be on January 15, and whether it may not even be the very date of my death!"

We shall find him, on this day, at Rome, wherein he had firmly resolved never to set foot. We shall see that it was exactly on January 15 that, in bravado and mockery, he allowed a Miraculous Medal to be hung about his neck. As he himself would write, "This marked the dawn of a new life for me."

From Strasbourg to Naples
(*November 1841–January 5, 1842*)

He set out on his journey toward the end of November. "As I quitted Strasbourg, I wept freely, for I was disturbed by an onrush of fears, by a thousand strange presentiments. When we completed the first stage of our journey, I was roused from my thoughts by sounds of merriment mingled with music on the roadside. Some village wedding party was leaving a church, to the sound of rustic flutes and violins. These country people surrounded my carriage as though they would invite me to join in their happiness. 'Soon enough, it will be my turn,' I said to myself, and this thought was enough to restore my good spirits."

The journey as planned was to last nine or ten months and included the following stops: Marseilles, where Alphonse was to take ship; Naples, where he was to stay for several weeks; then Malta, where he would spend a longer time; and finally Constantinople, whence he was to return to Strasbourg in time for the celebration of his wedding, set for the month of August 1842.

"I stayed for some days at Marseilles, being entertained by relatives and friends. It was almost impossible to tear myself away from their sumptuous hospitality. The very sea itself seemed intent upon refusing me passage, for it raised itself up in mountainous floods to bar my way, but finally these were trodden under by our steamer.

"Before arriving at Naples, the ship put in at Città Vecchia (the port of the Papal States). The cannon on the fort boomed loudly. In malign curiosity I enquired the meaning of these warlike sounds on the peaceful lands of the Pope. I was told 'This is the feast of the Conception of Our Lady.' I shrugged my shoulders, and did not disembark."

He thus made light of the Immaculate Virgin, as he was soon to do of the tears of Christ. On the following day, December 9, Alphonse reached Naples and found it enchanting. He wrote that he wanted "to see all there was to be seen in order to describe it all."

"As a matter of fact, what I did write was chiefly in criticism of religion and the clergy, for it seemed to me that in this delightful land they were out of place. How full of blasphemies is my journal! I wrote to Strasbourg that while on Vesuvius I had drunk of the *tears of Christ,* (Lacrima Christi wine) to the health of the Abbé Ratisbonne, and that these tears had agreed with me very well. I fear to transcribe other horrible examples of punning of which I was guilty.

"I had no wish whatever to visit Rome; and even though two Neapolitan friends of my family, M. Coulman who was a Protestant, and M. de Rothschild, tried to prevail upon me to agree to go there, I refused. Moreover, my fiancée had expressed the wish that I go at once to Malta, and she sent me instructions from my physician by which I was positively forbidden to go to Rome because of the prevalence, as he alleged, of fever in that city. Therefore, I had more than enough to deter me from such a visit, even had it been planned as part of my itinerary."

At Rome, by Error

But neither itinerary, fiancée, physician nor his own proposals proved availing! During the succeeding two weeks Ratisbonne was at the mercy of "chance" and outlandish impulses. We henceforth see him as a sort of somnambulist or automaton who was ruled by a stronger will than his own, a will which led him upon a road he was not himself inclined to take.

"I had booked passage on the *Mongibello* for Palermo." This is a Sicilian port from which one may reach Malta in a few hours. The *Mongibello* was scheduled to sail from Naples at the end of December.

"I was to leave with M. Vigne, a pleasant and respectable man whom I had met through M. Coulman. Like me, he was going to Malta. Pleased with this encounter, I said to myself: 'This friend has been sent me by heaven.' "

However — and this marks the first intervention of "chance" — the *Mongibello* broke down and remained in dock; and the travelers had to make arrangements to sail in another vessel departing on January 20.

"This New Year's Day was for me a very sad one. I was alone at Naples; no one sent me good wishes; no one was there whom I might clasp in my arms. I thought of my family, of the good wishes and celebrations of which my kind uncle was the center. I wept; and I found that the jolly manners of the Neapolitans only served to emphasize my grief.

"In search of distraction, I went out and followed mechanically the flow of the crowd. I came to the palace and found myself in front of a church without quite knowing how I had come there. I went in. I believe that Mass was being said. Whatever it was that was going on, I

stood against one of the pillars. My heart seemed to re-
spond in some way to these surroundings so strange to
me. I prayed in my own fashion, without paying attention
to what went on around me. I prayed for my fiancée, for
my uncle, for my dead father, and for the mother I had
lost while still so young; I prayed for all who were dear to
me; and I asked God to inspire and guide me in my plans
to help my fellow Jews, for this was a project which never
left my mind.

"The feeling of sadness now left me like a black cloud
dispelled by the wind. I felt an inward calm impossible
to describe but pervaded by a feeling of solace such as I
might experience had I heard a voice say: 'Your prayer
has been heard.' "

It would be at Rome that this deistic prayer would be
answered.

"But how did I go to Rome? This is all I can say, and I
find it impossible to explain it even to myself."

We now confront another "chance happening." "I must
have mistaken my direction, for instead of going to the
ticket office for Palermo to which I had set out, I found
myself at the place where carriages were taken for Rome.
I went in and paid my fare. I sent word to M. Vigne that I
could not forbear making a short excursion to Rome, but
that I should certainly return to Naples in time to set out,
as we had agreed, on January 20. This date was to mark
something quite different in my life.

"I left Naples on the fifth and reached Rome on the
sixth, the feast of the Three Kings. My traveling companion was an Englishman called Marshall, and I was
much entertained by his conversational originalities during the course of the journey.

"Rome did not convey to me, at first sight, the impres-

sion which I had sought. Having no more than a few days
to give to this unscheduled visit, I made a hasty effort to
gulp down, as it were, all the ancient and modern sights
which the city offers to the tourist. I crammed everything
pell-mell into my imagination and onto the pages of my
diary. In unchanging wonder, I rushed through art gal-
leries, circuses, churches, catacombs, through all the un-
numbered magnificences of Rome."

Never had the Eternal City seemed a more cosmopolitan
place than during those last years of the temporal power
of the Popes. Besides religious functions and artistic treasures, Rome offered select companions, a multitude of dis-
tractions, an infinitely agreeable life. Everyone enjoyed,
under the easy rule of the prelates appointed by the pontifical court, a degree of liberty unknown elsewhere in
Europe.

Among the foreigners who were then visiting Rome
were the Bussières, a Protestant family from Alsace, and
the Laferronays, Bréton Royalists, who were to play a
part in the miraculous events in which Ratisbonne became immersed.

The third "chance happening" now took place. "On
January 8 I heard someone calling me on the street; it
was a friend of my boyhood, Gustave de Bussières. I was
pleased at our meeting, for I was weary of being alone.
We dined with his father. Just as we entered the drawing
room, the elder son, M. Theodore de Bussières, came out.
I had never met him personally, but knew that he had
abandoned Protestantism to become a Catholic, and I
knew too that he was a friend of my brother Theodore.
This was enough to engender in me a deep dislike of him.
However, inasmuch as he was known for his writings on
the East and on Sicily, I thought that before going there

myself I might as well ask him about those places. Either for this reason or merely in order to be polite, I expressed the intention of calling upon him. He replied pleasantly, and added that he had just received a letter from the Abbé Ratisbonne, and that he would let me know my brother's new address. 'I shall be glad to have it,' I said to him, 'although I have no use for it.'

"We did not long remain talking, and when I left him I was annoyed at having committed myself to a visit which could only be useless and wasteful of my limited time.

"I continued to rush about Rome every day and all day long, except for two hours each morning which I spent with my friend Gustave, and for the relaxation I took each evening at the theater or in agreeable company. My meetings with Gustave were lively enough, for between two old school fellows, the thinnest memories are enough to arouse smiles and pleasantries. He was, however, a zealous Protestant, full of enthusiasm as are the Pietists at home in Alsace. He sought to impress me with the superiority of his own religious beliefs and he tried hard to convert me. This amused me very much, for until then I had believed that it was only Catholics who had this craze for convert-making. I answered him at all times in a light manner; but once, in order to please him, I told him that if ever I should become converted, I would make myself a Pietist. In return he made me a promise that in August he would attend my wedding."

The Roman Carnival, made immortal by Berlioz in his score of that name, was about to begin. It would last for eight days, from January 23 to 30. "M. Gustave de Bussières and two other friends of mine, M. Humann and M. Lotsbeck, made every effort to prevail upon me to delay my departure from Rome so that I might join in

these 'celebrations' which were without parallel elsewhere. But I was deaf to all their entreaties, for I feared
to displease my fiancée and I wanted to keep my promise
to M. Vigne who was waiting for me to set sail from
Naples on January 20, as I had told him I would.

"I had now but a few hours left in Rome. I took advantage of them to go to the Capitoline Hill where I
visited the Church of the Ara Coeli. Its impressive beauty
and the solemn music which resounded through its vast
interior, as well as the historical recollections which the
very ground aroused in me, all stirred me deeply. I was
moved, shaken, penetrated by the atmosphere, and this
was evident to my guide who looked at me coldly as he
remarked that it was not the first time that he had wit-
nessed such a reaction in a visitor to the Ara Coeli.

"As I went down from the Capitoline Hill, I had to
pass through the Ghetto. It was pity and indignation that
now overcame me. I asked myself, as I looked on the
wretched spectacle, if this was an example of that Roman
charity I had heard so vaunted. With a chill of horror I
wondered why the death of one man, eighteen hundred
years before, should be so visited on a whole people, and
I wondered, too, if they deserved treatment so barbarous
and restrictions so undying.

"I sent word to my family of what I had seen and felt.
I recall writing that I would prefer to be among the victims than with those who oppressed them. As I returned
to the Capitoline and regained sight of the Ara Coeli, I
noticed a good deal of activity, and on asking the reason
for these preparations I learned that two Jews, the brothers Constantini of Ancona, were to be baptized on the
morrow. I cannot express the indignation which filled me
when I heard this; and when my guide asked if I wished

to be present, I burst out: 'I? I attend so shameful a rite? No indeed, for I would not be able to restrain myself from throwing myself upon both baptizers and baptized.'

"Never before had I been so bitter against Christianity as after that visit to the Ghetto. I could not refrain from mockery and blasphemy.

"However, I still had some calls to make, and my promise to the Baron Theodore de Bussières recalled itself to me constantly as an unfortunate obligation which I had myself assumed. Very fortunately, however, I had neglected to obtain his address; and this seemed to me to settle the matter. I was delighted to have an excuse to avoid keeping my promise."

But in less than an hour, two further "chance happenings" occurred which spelt the ruin of this solution. Two servants figured in these incidents: the first accosted Ratisbonne without being sought; the second thrust him into a drawing room he did not wish to enter.

"It was January 15. I had reserved my place in the carriage going to Naples, and my departure was fixed for the 17th at three in the morning. I had but two more days, and I resolved to fill them in new ways. However, as I came out of a bookshop where I had been looking at some works dealing with Constantinople, I ran into a servant of the older M. de Bussières on the Corso; he greeted me, and I asked him for the address of the Baron Theodore de Bussières. In his Alsatian accent he replied: 'Number 38, Piazza Nicosia.'

"It appeared that, willy-nilly, I must make this call. Nevertheless, I told myself twenty times that I would not do it. Finally, I decided that the best way out of the situation would be to write p. p. c. on my card."

January 15: An Unwilling Visit
and a Medal Worn in Bravado

According to social usage, the letters p. p. c. (*pour prendre congé*, to take leave), written in the corner of a visiting card and left personally at the home of one's friends, served as a substitute for a visit. The letters p. p. c. would cover everything: they would testify that Ratisbonne had kept his word, and at the same time they would dispense him from the need of seeing one he wished to avoid. However, as it turned out, and once again as if by "chance," p. p. c. helped him not at all.

It was an Italian servant who answered the door. Being ignorant alike of French and of French social customs, he left the visitor standing with his card in his hand and hastening into the salon to announce him, he hurried Ratisbonne into the room.

"I hid my chagrin as best I could by attempting to smile, and I went to sit near Madame la Baronne de Bussières. She was in the company of her two young daughters, pretty and sweet as Raphael's angels. Our conversation was at first light and pointless, but soon became marked with feeling as I began to give my impressions of Rome.

"I looked upon the Baron de Bussières as being devout in the bad sense of that word, and I was pleased at having an opportunity of dilating upon the conditions which afflicted the Jews in Rome. This comforted me, but it resulted in fixing the conversation upon religious subjects. M. de Bussières spoke to me of the grandeur of Catholicism; I responded with irony and with some of the sarcastic barbs I had so often heard or read, although I was careful to keep a check upon my impious wit in deference to Madame de Bussières and for the sake of the little children who were playing nearby."

As Bussières tells us in his *Journal*, Ratisbonne was not able to restrain himself in speaking of the Ghetto; he declared that this "dreadful sight had aroused all his latent hatred of Catholicism. I sought to lead him to share my own convictions; but he laughed at my efforts, and in a spirit of benevolent pity for my superstition he declared: 'A Jew was I born, and a Jew shall I die.'

" 'Well then, since you are so strong-minded and so sure of yourself,' I said to him, 'promise me to wear something I am going to give you.'

" 'We shall see. What do you mean?'

" 'It is only a medal.'

"And I showed him a Miraculous Medal. In a combination of indignation and surprise, he thrust it vigorously aside. 'But,' I said, 'as you look at things, this should be an indifferent matter in your eyes, while it will give me a great deal of pleasure.'

" 'Oh! it is really but a small matter,' he cried out laughingly; 'and at least I can show you how wrong it is to say that the Jews are obstinate and headstrong. Moreover, this will give me material for something to say in my letters and in my account of my travels.' He added much more in a joking style which pierced my heart, for to me his jokes were blasphemous."

Alphonse Ratisbonne takes up the narrative again with the avowal: "I agreed to accept the medal as a bit of evidence to be offered to my fiancée.

"No sooner was this agreed to, than it was accomplished. The medal was placed about my neck with some effort, for the ribbon was rather short. Finally, by forcing it over my head, I had the medal on my breast, and I burst out laughing as I exclaimed: 'Ah! ha! I am now become Catholic, Apostolic, and Roman.'

"It was the devil who prophesied through my mouth. M. de Bussières took a simple pleasure in his victory, and he tried to take advantage of it.

" 'Now,' he said to me, 'you must not shirk the rest. Each morning and evening you must say the *Memorare,* a very short and effective prayer written by St. Bernard in honor of Our Lady.' [2]

" 'What is this *Memorare* of which you speak?' I burst out. 'Enough of such foolishness, please.' For at this instant all my animosity had awakened. The mention of St. Bernard recalled my brother, for he had written the life of this saint, a book I had no wish to read. And these thoughts in turn lent fire to all my distaste for proselytism, Jesuitry, and those whom I called Tartufes and apostates.[3] I begged M. de Bussières to let the matter rest, and full of the spirit of mockery as I was, I expressed regret that I could not equalize matters by offering him, in return, some Hebrew prayer; but I did not know any.

"Wishing to treat the whole affair lightly, I said: 'Very well! I promise that I will say your prayer; if it does me no good, at least it will not do me any harm!' M. de Bussières found the prayer and asked me to copy it. I agreed, but on the condition 'that I keep your original, and give you my copy.' It was my thought that in this way I would increase my collection of souvenirs with another bit of evidence.

2 Although the attribution of the *Memorare* to St. Bernard has long been traditional, it is not now regarded as being accurate.

3 A few years prior to this time, Theodore Ratisbonne had written his *Vie de Saint Bernard* in two volumes, and it had enjoyed some success. Alphonse here employs "jesuitisme" or "jesuitry" in the pejorative sense made famous by Pascal which had passed into some European dictionaries as a synonym for "disingenuous."

"We were completely satisfied with each other; the encounter seemed to me outlandish, but it had amused me. When we parted, I went to the theater and forgot both medal and *Memorare*. But when I came home from the theater I found a note from M. de Bussières who had come to my hotel, the Serny, to return my call. He invited me to see him again before I left Rome. I stood obliged, in any event, to restore his *Memorare* to him, and before it was time to leave on the 17th at three in the morning, I finished my packing, and then set about copying the prayer:

"Remember, O most gracious Virgin Mary, that never was it known that anyone who fled to thy protection, implored thy help, or sought thy intercession was left unaided. Inspired by this confidence, I fly unto thee, O Virgin of virgins my Mother. To thee I come: before thee I stand, sinful and sorrowful. O Mother of the Word Incarnate, despise not my petitions, but graciously hear and answer me. Amen.

"Mechanically, I copied out these words almost without attending to what I was doing. I was overtired, the hour was late, and I was in need of rest."

From January 16 to 19

Although his packing was completed, Alphonse still dallied in deference to Bussières for all that he considered him a chatterer, a friend of the Abbé Ratisbonne and his Jesuits, "a superstitious Catholic marked with a mania for convert-making," in sum, a perfect example of all those religious hypocrites and canting humbugs whom he so disliked. Not only did he defer to Bussières, he seems to have been quite unable to leave the tiresome baron who had done so much that inclined Ratisbonne to fly from Rome. He actually spent several hours with him each day. We seem to be dealing here with a real sleepwalker!

On Sunday, January 16, Alphonse wrote: "Today I secured my visa and I finished my preparations for leaving, all the while repeating the *Memorare*. How had it happened that those words had made so powerful an impression on my mind? They recurred to me ceaselessly, as some musical phrases do, pursuing and importuning and, as it seems, insisting on being hummed over and over.

"At about eleven o'clock, I went to call on M. de Bussières to return to him his everlastingly persistent prayer. I talked of my trip to the Orient, and he gave me much useful information.

"However, he suddenly burst out with these words: 'How peculiar it is of you to leave Rome now, just as everyone is preparing to attend the solemnities in celebration of St. Peter's Chair which will be held tomorrow with the Pope presiding in the basilica of the Vatican. Perhaps you may never return to Rome, and surely you will regret having missed a sight which many come from such distances to see.'

"I answered that I had already reserved and paid for my passage; that I had informed my family of my plans; that letters awaited me at Palermo; that, after all, it was too late to change all these arrangements; and that, in any event, I was resolved to go. This conversation was interrupted by the arrival of the post which included a letter from the Abbé Ratisbonne to M. de Bussières. He showed it to me, and I read it without being interested in it. This unlooked-for incident served to curtail my visit, for the mere thought of my brother was enough to put me to flight. Nevertheless, for some inexplicable reason, I made up my mind to prolong my stay in Rome, thus yielding to the importunities of a man I scarcely knew, although I had obstinately refused to listen to my most intimate friends.

We have spoken of Ratisbonne as behaving like a somnambulist or an automaton. For a moment he now interrupts his own account of events in order to expose the truth of the matter.

"What then," he cries out, "what then, O my God, was this irresistible force that led me against my own wishes? From Strasbourg I was driven to Italy despite the invitations I had received from Valencia and from Paris. From Naples I was impelled to go to Rome, notwithstanding my determination to proceed to Sicily. Finally, in Rome, when I was ready to leave, what forced me to pay a visit which repelled me at the very time that I could not find an opportunity to visit those whom I would have been happy to see? . . . How providential was Your leading of me! . . .

"I had intended only to spend the time of the carnival at Rome, but I did want to see the Pope, and here was the Baron de Bussières giving me his word that I should see him at St. Peter's on the eighteenth. We took some drives together, we discussed what we saw, structures, paintings, customs. Into everything M. de Bussières managed to introduce religion, and he did this so openly and labored it so strongly that more than once it occurred to me that nothing could so indispose a man to religion as this sort of attempt to convert him to it. However, my natural frivolity led me to find laughing matter in the most serious subjects, and to the outbursts of my wit were joined the hellish fire of my blasphemies, something which I no longer dare to remember. These journeys by carriage lasted one or two hours, and they continued for the two following days."

Bussières tells us that going on Sunday evening to the Palazzo Borghese to dine with the Comte de Laferronays,[4] he spoke of his "current project" and earnestly commended "the young Israelite to the count's prayers." " 'Do not worry,' replied Laferronays, 'if you have him saying the *Memorare*, you already have him fast!' "

M. de Bussières' *Journal* continues:

"*Monday, January 17.* Another drive with Ratisbonne. It was with vexation that I noted how little result our conversations have had: his feelings remain as before; he is hostile toward Catholicism, unable to say a good word for it, but striving to escape by sallies of wit from arguments which he will not take the trouble to refute.

"Last night, M. de Laferronays died suddenly at about eleven o'clock. His friends, who had been so inspired by his fervor during his last years, believed that God had called him because he deserved heaven. I myself had loved him as a father, and I shared with his family in the sadness of this unhappy parting. Yet even by the bier of my friend I was haunted by thoughts of Ratisbonne.

"*Tuesday, 18.* I spent part of the night with the bereaved family, and I hesitated to leave them. Nevertheless, my disturbed thoughts were ceaselessly turning back to Ratisbonne. . . . I again went about with him, seeking to subdue him by linking up Catholic truth to the religious

---

[4] The Comte de Laferronays (1777–1842), who had been in the French Ministry during the Restoration and had a reputation as a diplomat, had taken part in the congresses of Toppau, Laybach and Verona.

antiquities upon which we gazed in our tours of the city; but I spoke in vain."

He had, first of all, taken Ratisbonne to the Gesu, the church of the Jesuits, where as if by chance they found Père de Villefort. As he was Bussières' confessor, it is likely that the encounter had been prearranged. Making use of a tactic which is sometimes successful, Père de Villefort tried to carry the day by direct assault. "Down upon your knees; let us join in prayer," he said to Ratisbonne. He, however, categorically refused this invitation and went out more than ever indisposed toward Jesuits.

Bussières wanted him to go again to the Ara Coeli where the week before Ratisbonne had been so favorably impressed. Alphonse suffered himself to be led there like a sheep, but on this occasion he felt nothing whatever: "He [Ratisbonne] heard what I had to say coldly and replied to all my reflections by witticisms. 'I will recall this when I am at Malta,' he said. 'I will have plenty of time, for I shall be there for two months. It will serve to banish my boredom.' "

"*Wednesday, January 19.* This time I directed our course to Monte Celio, where stands the Church of Saint Stephen with its frescoes showing the sufferings of the martyrs. These aroused in Ratisbonne only horror: 'This is a monstrous sight,' he cried out before I could say anything, 'but your co-religionists were themselves as cruel in their treatment of the poor Jews as ever were the pagan persecutors of the early Christians.' When we parted, I failed to carry away even the slightest hope of having in the least changed his mind."

Alphonse tells us that it was at some time on this Wednesday that Bussières had said to him:

" 'Despite all your lack of patience with what I have to

say, I am convinced that you will one day be a Christian, for you are basically so just that I believe that you will come to the light of truth even though it mean that the Lord must visit you by His heavenly angel.'

"My reply was to declare, 'That is the only way in which what you hope for can ever come about.'

"Passing by the *Scala Sancta,* M. de Bussières became quite enthusiastic. He stood up in the carriage and taking off his hat, he cried out excitedly: 'Hail, holy staircase! Behold before you a sinner who will one day mount you on his knees!' It would be impossible to express the effect which was produced upon me by his thus paying honor to a flight of steps. I laughed at it as a wholly senseless act, and when later we approached the lovely Villa Wolkonski, with its flowering gardens intersected by the Neronian aqueducts, in my turn I raised my voice and parodying my friend I exclaimed: 'Hail, true wonders of God's hand! It is rather to you than to a flight of steps that homage is due!' "

Ratisbonne noted that on this day, as on the day before, Bussières seemed sad, depressed and generally less talkative than usual. Not knowing the cause of his sorrow, he ascribed the baron's silence to some feeling of discouragement at his own lack of response to Bussières' efforts to convert him. "I even thought that he had forgotten his medal, although I was myself, even if in the spirit of complete impatience, forever saying over to myself the unforgettable words of St. Bernard."

The Night of January 18 and the Morning of January 20

Yet, he thought happily, he would not much longer be in this state of durance. He was obligated to wear the

medal and to say the *Memorare* only while he remained
in Rome, and his visit was drawing to a close. The time
was coming to yield to the wishes of his fiancée and to
rejoin M. Vigne. The latter had informed him of the
sailing of another vessel, and this time Alphonse was
ready to go at once.

"My departure was finally set for the 22nd, and once
again I reserved a place in the Naples coach. However,
in the night between the 19th and the 20th, I awakened
with a start and saw before me a large cross of a special
shape without the body of Christ being attached to it."
Later, he was to identify this cross with the cross of the
Miraculous Medal.

"I made attempt after attempt to dispel this picture,
but I was unable to avoid it, for turn as I might from side
to side, it was ever before me. I cannot say how long this
lasted. Finally, I fell asleep again; and the next morning
on awakening, I thought no more of it.

"I had some letters to write, and I recall that I ended
one of these, which was addressed to my fiancée's younger
sister, with the words: 'May God keep you.' Later I was
to receive from my fiancée herself a letter also dated
January 20, and to find that she, as well, had concluded
with the words: 'May God keep you.' That day was really
a day in God's keeping. Nevertheless, had anyone told me
on the morning of this day: 'You have awakened as a Jew,
but it is as a Christian that you shall sleep this night,' I
would have looked upon him as the most arrant of fools.

"I breakfasted at my hotel and took my letters to the
post office. Then I went to visit my friend, Gustave de
Bussières, the Pietist, who had for some days been absent
from the city on a hunting trip. He was most astonished
to find me still in Rome, and I explained that it was my
wish to see the Pope that had detained me.

" 'However, I shall, all the same, go away without having seen him,' I remarked, 'for he did not assist at the ceremonies held on the feast of St. Peter's Chair, where I had hoped I might have sight of him.'

"Gustave consoled me, in ironic fashion, by talking of another ceremony, a rather strange one, which I understood would take place at Santa Maria Maggiore. It was the blessing of the animals. And it may be imagined what puns and low pleasantries were exchanged upon this subject between a Jew and a Protestant.

"We parted at about eleven o'clock, promising to meet again on the morrow, and I went to a café in the Piazza di Spagna where I might see the papers. I had but arrived when M. Edmond Humann came to sit beside me. We spoke lightly of Paris, of artistic and political matters. Soon, another friend, M. Alfred de Lotsbeck, approached me, and with him I had an even more discursive chat. We spoke of hunting, of pleasure, of the jollity of the carnival which was about to begin, and of the wonderful party which the Duke of Torlonia had given the night before. I could not refrain from referring to my own wedding, and I invited M. de Lotsbeck who promised me that he would be there.

"If a third person had then come up and said to me: 'Alphonse, in one quarter of an hour you will adore Jesus Christ as your God and Saviour. You will be on your knees in a poor little church. At the feet of a priest, in a house of the Jesuits, you will strike your breast in acknowledgment of sin. You will be ready to die for the Catholic Faith. You will turn your back on the world and its delights, on your fortune, your hopes, your future. If need be, you will be prepared to give up even your fiancée, the love of your family, the good opinion of your friends,

your sense of solidarity with your people. . . . You will
think only of following Jesus Christ, of sharing in his
Cross, until you die' . . . I say that if anyone had come
before me with this prophecy I would have thought him
the maddest of men, one whose folly could be exceeded
only by that of anyone who would believe in the mere
possibility of such nonsense ever coming to pass."

At this time Bussières came up, and he has recorded
that: "Ratisbonne had not advanced one step in the direction of the truth. His nature is to mock; his thoughts are
ever bent on things of the earth. At the Café d'Espagne,
where he had met my brother-in-law Humann, he spoke
to him of topics of the day in a manner so frivolous as to
exclude any seriousness whatsoever."

The Apparition of January 20

"When I emerged from the café," writes Alphonse, "the
carriage of M. de Bussières was passing. He stopped and
invited me to join him in a drive. The day was beautiful,
and I assented with pleasure. M. de Bussières asked if
I would mind his leaving me for a few minutes at the
Church of Sant' Andrea delle Frate, which was quite near
and where he had an errand to do. He suggested that
I await him in the carriage; but I preferred to get out in
order to see the church.

"Within preparations were being made for a funeral.
I asked for whom this was to be. He replied, 'For one of
my friends, the Comte de Laferronays. His sudden death
is the reason for the depression you may have noted in
me these past two days.'

"I had not known M. de Laferronays; and I felt only
that vague discomfort which is always aroused by the news

of a sudden death. M. de Bussières left me in order to
visit a tribune reserved for the family of the dead man.
'Do not be impatient,' he said as he went to this private
section of the church; 'I shall be no more than a few
minutes.'

"The Church of Sant' Andrea seemed to me small, poor
and forgotten; I felt as if I were alone in it. There were
no works of art to draw my attention. I walked about
aimlessly, without seeing anything to arouse a thought.
I can recall only that a black dog sprang into my path . . .
but soon he was gone. Then the church itself seemed to
disappear; and I saw nothing at all. . . . Or I should rather
say, O my God, that I saw one thing alone!

"How can I speak of this? No! human words cannot
even try to convey what is beyond expression. . . . When
M. de Bussières recalled me to myself, I was in tears and
was unable to answer his questions. . . . But I seized the
medal which was on my breast and I fervently kissed
the image of the Virgin. . . . Oh! it had indeed been
she! . . . I did not know where I was; I did not know if
I were Alphonse or someone else. I felt so deep a change
in me that I believed myself to be another; I sought to
regain my consciousness of self, and I could not. . . . I was
not able to speak; I did not wish to discuss what had happened; I felt within myself something so solemn and so
sacred as to require me to ask for a priest."

Bussières tells us: "My absence had been a matter of
no more than ten or twelve minutes at the most. Ratisbonne had begun by walking about in the nave and his
cold and indifferent look seemed to say, 'What an ugly
church this is!' When I left him he was at the Epistle
side, to the right of the little enclosure which had been prepared for the coffin of the Comte de Laferronays.

"When I returned, I did not at once see Ratisbonne; but then I found him on his knees before St. Michael's chapel. I went up to him, and I had to touch him three or four times before he realized that I was there. Finally, he turned to me a face covered with tears; he joined his hands and said in a way I cannot describe: 'Ah! how this man has prayed for me!'

"I was myself quite stupefied with astonishment; I felt as if I were in the presence of the miraculous. I assisted Ratisbonne to get up, and I led him, almost carrying him, from the church. I asked what had happened, or where he wished to go.

" 'Take me wherever you wish,' he cried; 'after what I have seen, I will obey.'

"I urged him to explain, but he could not; he was too upset. He kept on kissing the Miraculous Medal which was wet with his tears. I brought him back to his hotel, but despite all my efforts all I could get out of him were exclamations, interspersed with sobs.

" 'Ah!' he said, 'how happy I am! How good God is! How great are the graces of happiness! How we should pity those who do not know this!'

"Then he burst into tears. . . . Finally, he asked me if he were mad; but then he at once cried out: 'No, indeed, I am not mad. My God! My God! I am not mad. All the world knows it.'

"When this delirium of feeling began to abate, Ratisbonne, his face shining with joy, grasped my arm and asked me to take him to a confessor so that he might learn when he could be baptized, saying that otherwise he did not know how he would continue to live. He was envious of the sufferings of the martyrs which he had seen depicted at the Church of San Stefano in Rotondo. He declared that he would not explain himself until after he had obtained permission to do so from a priest. 'For,' he added, 'what I have to say can only be said when I am on my knees.'

"I took him immediately to the Church of the Gesu, to Père de Villefort, who tried to draw an explanation from him. Ratisbonne again grasped his medal, and kissing it, he said: 'I have seen her! I have seen her! . . .' And once more he was overcome by emotion. However, he became calmer and he finished by explaining himself. These are his own words:

" 'I had been in that church for only a very brief time when all at once I felt myself in the grip of a disturbance impossible to describe. I raised my eyes; I could no longer see anything of the building. All the light seemed as if it were concentrated in one of the chapels, and in the midst of its shining there stood upon the altar the Virgin Mary as she is shown on the medal, beautiful, glorious, and embodying at once both majesty and kindness. A force which I could not resist drew me toward her. The Virgin made a sign with her hand that I should kneel and she seemed to say: "It is well." She did not actually speak to me, but I understood as if she had.'

"In giving us this brief description, Ratisbonne interrupted himself frequently as though to catch his breath and to master his emotions. We listened with a blessed dread in which joy was mingled."

Here then is the full description of the Apparition of Our Lady on Thursday, January 20, 1842: she showed herself for a moment and made a gesture with her hand.

Bussières continues his narrative: "Ratisbonne and I left Père de Villefort to go to give thanks to God, first at Santa Maria Maggiore and then at St. Peter's.

" 'Ah!' he declared with a degree of elevation I cannot convey, 'how good it is to be in this church.' He pressed my hand and he said: 'One seems to be no longer on earth, but as if in Heaven. I wish that I never needed to leave here.'

"He not only believed in the Real Presence; he felt its reality. When he was approaching the altar of reservation, he seemed quite overcome and as though he ought at once to withdraw, for it seemed to him a horrible thing to come before the living God in the state of original sin. He went to take refuge in the chapel of Our Lady, saying, 'Here, at least, I am not fearful, for I know myself to be under the protection of boundless mercy.' "

Bussières took Ratisbonne back to the Hotel Serny, and then left him so that he might hasten to tell the great news to the Laferronays family.

"However, Ratisbonne had begged me not to leave him alone, and I came back to him as soon as possible. I asked for more details about his vision. He was unable to explain how, from the right side of the church where I had left him, he had passed to St. Michael's chapel, which is at the left, and was on the other side of the place which had been prepared for the funeral service. He had suddenly found himself on his knees before this chapel which, as a matter of fact, contained neither painting nor statue of the Blessed Virgin. Immediately, he was able to distinguish the Queen of Heaven in all her beauteous splendor. And it was no mere image that he saw: 'It was she herself that I beheld, in reality; I saw her just as I now see you!' But his eyes were unable to bear the brightness of this heavenly light. Three times he tried to look at her face again; but each time he was unable to raise his eyes beyond her hands from whence there poured, just as on the medal, torrents of grace in the appearance of rays of light."

From Friday, January 21, to Sunday, January 30

On the following day, which was Friday, there took place at the Church of Sant' Andrea delle Frate the funeral of the Comte de Laferronays. A rumor soon circulated among the distinguished assemblage who were in attendance at the ceremony that a miracle had taken place in the church. In order to avoid the general curiosity thus aroused, Ratisbonne left the Hotel Serny and took refuge at the home of Bussières. He remained in retirement there for three days, only going out to see Père de Villefort at the Church of the Gesu.

He wrote to his fiancée, to his uncle, to the Abbé Theodore, to his other brothers and sisters, and to the long-suffering M. Vigne who continued patiently to await his arrival at Naples. He was happier than he could say. The one thing that disturbed him was the thought of his relatives. He had begun to hope that they too would be converted under the influence of the wonders that it had been granted him to see.

"They know me," he said to Bussières; "they know very well that I am no fool, that I have never been one. They will not forget that I have the best of reasons for remaining a Jew like my fiancée, my uncle and my family. They know that my whole future lies with the Jews. They must trust me."

Nevertheless, he rather foresaw that they would regard him as foundering in madness; and this realization terrified him. He resolved to disappear for good from the society of men.

"I bound my confessor, Père de Villefort, and M. de Bussières to keep inviolate the secret of what had happened to me. I felt that my family and my friends would think me insane and would mock me. So I wished to hide myself among the Trappists in order to avoid the scorn of the worldly."

Père de Villefort dared not assume the responsibility of consenting to this, and he called upon the general of the Society of Jesus for counsel. He received them in his quarters and "both priests," as Ratisbonne tells us, "pointed out to me that ridicule, unjust judgment, injuries to my reputation were all part of the chalice of a true Christian. They urged me to drink of it."

After he had questioned Alphonse at length, the father general showed him a crucifix upon his writing table. "Once you have been baptized," he said, "you must not only adore this Cross which was shown to you during your sleep; you must carry it as well." Then he opened his Bible, and from the Book of Ecclesiasticus he read these verses:

"Son, when thou comest to the service of God, stand in justice and in fear, and prepare thy soul for temptation. Humble thy heart, and endure: incline thy ear, and receive the words of understanding: and make not haste in the time of clouds. Wait on God with patience: join thyself to God, and endure, that thy life may be increased in the latter end. Take all that shall be brought upon thee: and in thy sorrow endure, and in thy humiliation keep patience. For gold and silver are tried in the fire, but acceptable men in the furnace of humiliation. Believe God, and he will recover thee: and direct thy way, and trust in him. Keep his fear, and grow old therein" (2:1–6).

Alphonse copied out this passage that he might reread

it and think about it each day of his life. "I was not dis-
couraged by these serious words; they rather served to
increase my joy that flamed more ardently within me; I
felt ready for all I might be called upon to bear, and I
begged earnestly for Baptism. They wished to defer it.
'Why so?' I exclaimed. 'The Jews who heard the preaching of the Apostles were baptized immediately, and you
want to put me off after I have "heard" the preaching of
the Queen of the Apostles.' My feelings and my urgent
wishes, my pleadings touched the hearts of these kind men
who had befriended me, and it was promised that I should
be baptized."

It was decided that Alphonse would receive Baptism,
together with Confirmation and the Holy Eucharist, after
making a retreat at the Gesu from January 23–30. Most
certainly, it was unusual to proceed so hastily. But this
was a case hitherto unheard of. By a simple sign that
declared "It is well," Our Lady had at once changed his
heart and enlightened his mind.

"All my anti-Christian prejudices had vanished, leaving
not the least trace. At the sign given by Our Lady a veil
had fallen from my eyes, or rather I should say I was relieved of all the veils which had surrounded me; for they
fell quickly and one after another just as the snow melts
before the rays of the bright sun.

"I had come out of a dark pit, out of a tomb . . . and
I was alive, completely alive. . . . I thought of my brother
Theodore with inexpressible joy. But how I wept as I
thought of my family, of my fiancée, of my poor sisters.
I wept indeed, as I thought of them whom I so loved
and for whom I said the first of my prayers. . . . Will
you not raise your eyes to the Saviour whose blood blots
out original sin? Oh! how hideous is the mark of this

taint, and how does it alter beyond recognition the creature made in God's own likeness!"

How remarkable it is to find in Ratisbonne this almost
physical horror of original sin, "a belief entirely forgotten
by the Jews of the day, something indeed of which I had
never thought." It is true that he has just been confronted
with the Immaculate Conception of Our Lady. Other
dogmas he knew as well; and he felt convinced of them,
believing in the Trinity, in the Incarnation, in salvation
dependent on the merits of Christ, in the Eucharist, and
in the Communion of Saints.

"I knew most certainly that M. de Laferronays had
prayed for me. How did I know it? I cannot say; but no
more can I explain how I learned all the other truths
of which I now had knowledge. And I had never opened
any books dealing with religion; nor had I read a single
page from the Bible. All that I can say is that when I
went into the Church of Sant' Andrea I knew nothing;
when I came out all was clear to me.

"So from henceforth the world means nothing to me;
the love of God has so wholly encompassed all other love
that I think of even my fiancée herself in a different
light. Now I love her as something precious in the hands
of God and as a reason for loving all the more that God
from whom she came."

Once again he wrote to her during his retreat. These
six lines are all that remain to us of the letters which
passed between these two who had loved so long and so
much.

"Eight days ago had some sudden misfortune forced me
to renounce you, I would have lost courage and would
have taken my life. . . . Today, should my newly found
belief sunder us, I could offer God this sacrifice without

a tear; and all my life I would pray that he might en-lighten you and reunite us in heaven."

The ceremony of the abjuration of error was set for Monday, January 31, in the Church of the Gesu, and Cardinal Patrizzi officiated. We have, from one who was present at it, a description of the function in these terms:

"The catechumen [i.e. Ratisbonne] was clad in a long robe of white silk, and he waited in the back of the church behind a barrier marking off the holy place. The cardinal came to him in procession, and the exorcism began.

" 'What do you ask?'

" 'Baptism.'

" 'What, then, do you wish?'

" 'Life eternal.'

" 'Do you renounce Satan?'

" 'I do renounce him.'

" 'Do you believe in Jesus Christ?'

" 'I do believe in him.'

"Mere formularies were transcended. The young man's brief replies were firm and energetic as he gazed straight-forwardly yet modestly at the prelate who asked the ques-tions. From the noble firmness of his bearing, the almost unstirred calmness of his face which scarcely showed a variation from its natural pallor — from all these marks of a carefully reflective character, one sensed the courage of a man who had won a victory over the most inveterate part of his whole nature: the earliest and most deep-sealed ties of his heart. One sigh of inexpressible happiness did escape him, and a smile was on his lips as he lifted up his head from the waters of the baptismal font.

"Now the barrier was cast down and the neophyte was led before the altar, through immense throngs of people

who respectfully made way for him. Here the cardinal
conferred on him the sacrament of Confirmation. As the
gifts of the Holy Spirit descended upon him he seemed to
humble himself beneath them."

One of the great orators of the era, the Abbé Dupan-
loup, thus describes the conclusion of the ceremonial:
"Mass was then said, and during it Ratisbonne received
his first Communion. He went before the altar to receive
the sacred host. This last grace seemed to cause his soul
to overflow. Until now he had been entirely the master
of his emotion, but at this point he was unable to control
the strange new feeling of happiness that welled up within
him, and all at once he burst into sobs and had to be
supported, half-fainting, back to his place."

From His Conversion until His Death (1842–1884)

The Church is usually cautious about a conversion,
for the reason that no one can be certain of the future
role of the convert, especially if he be young and in good
health. Nevertheless, the events of January 20 aroused so
much interest at Rome and in France that a Roman court
of inquiry was immediately convened. The hearings lasted
until June 3, at which time a pontifical decree was published stating "that it is certain that a true and notable
miracle, the work of God, through the intercession of the
Blessed Virgin, did produce the instantaneous and complete conversion of Alphonse Ratisbonne."

These are the same terms that the breviary was to take
up and incorporate into the Office of the Miraculous
Medal. As we have seen, the conversion was instantaneous; what is to follow will show it to have been complete.

"Letters from my family left me at liberty to do as I

wished," Alphonse wrote on April 12, 1842. In other words, he lost his inheritance, and he was denied by his own; he lost, as well, his fiancée, and in addition he saw her who had been a deist turn again into an atheist.

In June 1842, the same month in which the Roman decree was published, he entered the Society of Jesus. Here he remained for six years. Finally, he withdrew from the Jesuits in order to join his brother Theodore in the foundation of the Congregation of the Priests and Ladies of Sion. Their work was to be the conversion of the Jews.

The two brothers divided world responsibility between them: to the older was assigned the care of the West and the establishment of institutions in France, in England, in Austria and in Romania; to the younger was given the Orient, together with Constantinople and the Holy Places. He who had been favored with the apparition of Our Lady in Sant' Andrea delle Frate was now Père Marie-Alphonse, and he acquired the ruins of the praetorium of Pontius Pilate and made three foundations in Jerusalem: the Ecce Homo, Saint John in Montana, and the College of Saint Peter.

He was in need of funds to support these foundations, and out of love for his fellow Jews, the one-time dandy became a beggar. He was himself typically Jewish in his appearance, and as he went about with his long beard he seemed like some high priest of the Old Law. He was always merry and kind, and he gave generously to all of his own interior happiness as he sought to obtain their charity.

For many years he traveled through Spain, France, Belgium, England, Austria and Germany. At times he was well received; at others harshly rebuffed. In London he was once invited to attend a party with the promise that he would encounter many generous people who would be interested in his work. He found that it was into the center of a ballroom that he had been taken, and there they mocked him. While in Paris he was summoned before the archbishop's officials as being suspected of soliciting funds for a non-existent sanctuary.

He was endowed with the directness of a child and with remarkable humility. One day he asked his great friend Père Estrade, "Can you understand why it was that the Virgin appeared to a being like myself, and why it was to me that she pointed out the congregation which her divine Son wished to see established?"

Père Estrade rose and looked directly at Ratisbonne.

"Yes; I understand it," he said.

"Do you know *why?*"

"Why? It was because in choosing an instrument as unworthy as yourself she knew that naught of the glory due to God would be deflected upon the instrument; that all glory would return to the Author of all good."

"Ah," said Père Marie-Alphonse delightedly, "this is a point of view that had escaped me. I will take care not to forget it."

On the details of the miracle he remained reserved and mysterious. Following the canonical inquiry, it was only to the Comte de Chambord,[5] to Père Estrade, and to two or three intimate friends that he ever spoke of the vision. His friend, Mère Stouhlen, foundress of the Ladies of Sion, said to him on one occasion:

"I should like to ask you a question. Will you answer it?"

[5] The Comte de Chambord (1820–1883), grandson of Charles X and pretender to the throne of France, was the last of the French Bourbons.

"Gladly."

"Do you still see the Blessed Virgin?"

"She is more and more lovely," he said; and then he bowed his head.

He was even more reticent on the subject of the interior trials from which he suffered so long and so bitterly. Yet we know that he did drink the chalice of tribulation which had been predicted to him, and that the great cross which was shown him on the night of January 20 was grievous to bear.

On May 6, 1884, he died in Jerusalem. His last words, "All my wishes have been granted!" were spoken in response to someone who had asked him how he felt.

Did Our Lady manifest herself to him at that last moment? According to those who watched by him, "at about eight o'clock in the evening, a light shone upon his face, and he opened his eyes which had been hitherto continually closed. They seemed full of life, and they expressed at first surprise and then delight. This appearance of ecstasy lasted for three minutes. Then he gently dropped his lids and effortlessly and quietly gave up his soul to God. He seemed to be peacefully asleep, and it was a long while before any sign of death appeared upon his face."

Flore Ratisbonne (1825–1915)

And what of his little fiancée, the girl of sixteen so fearful of the effects of the Roman climate on her future husband, and whom he had promised, as she went from him, that he would keep ever in his prayers and would ever hope for their reunion in heaven?

Although the conversion of Alphonse was, as the Roman Breviary says, "instantaneous," that of Flore required more time. As we learn from Abbé Klein's book on Madeleine Semer,[6] time ran on for three-quarters of a century. On October 30, 1912, Madeleine Semer, a young divorcée who had been married to a prominent member of the French Chamber of Deputies, was in search of employment in Paris. She applied to an elderly woman who engaged her as a secretary and reader, and who soon came to treat her as a friend.

Madame Singer, formerly Flore Ratisbonne, was then in her eighty-eighth year. She had retained all the brilliance of mind and the goodness of heart that had won her so many friends. In the days of the Second Empire such figures as Prévost-Paradol, Octave Feuillet, Caro, Émile Ollivier had been among those who came to her home. It was still a focus of noted visitors in 1912, and their stature had in no way lessened. Now the guests included Brunetière, Paul Deschanel, Prince Albert de Monaco, and they visited her regularly.[7] It was at Madame Singer's that Madeleine Semer discussed philosophical matters with Bergson and set out upon that path of development which brought her soul from unbelief to Christian mysticism.

Madame Singer herself was always held back by the

[6] Félix Klein, *Madeleine Semer, convertie et mystique, 1874–1921.* 28th ed. (Paris, 1929).

[7] Prévost-Paradol (1829–1870), writer and journalist. Napoléon III had hopes of securing the intervention of the United States in the War of 1870 on the side of France, and he sent Prévost-Paradol to Washington to this end; but he committed suicide at the French Embassy shortly after his arrival there. Octave Feuillet (1821–1890), novelist and playwright. Elme-Marie Caro (1826–1887), philosopher and moralist. Émile Ollivier (1825–1913), son-in-law of Liszt and brother-in-law of Wagner, he was President of the Council of State in France at the time of the War of 1870. Ferdinand Brunetière (1849–1906), literary critic. Paul Deschanel (1885–1922), President of the French Republic. Prince Albert of Monaco (1848–1922), a distinguished expert in oceanography. Henri Bergson (1851–1944), a philosopher of Polish antecedents who became a naturalized Frenchman.

problem of evil: its existence kept her from believing in God. In her words of leave-taking to Madeleine Semer, as they are found in her will, we read these suggestions of atheism: "You are well aware of my limited budget, and you know, my very dear friend, that I am not able to cover you with gold as you indeed deserve. But I yet feel that the life-long gratitude I feel toward you will be truly valued by you. In the most considerate and most consistent fashion you have unfailingly been at my side to help me bear my constant sufferings. If you have not been able to win me to belief in God, Father of all mankind, I nevertheless do believe in his angels; for you have been a slave to duty and an angel of mercy."

However, when Madame Singer finally died on November 25, 1915, she had been in the habit for three months of asking Madeleine Semer to recite the evening prayer aloud in her presence each night. And on the last night of her life, while perfectly lucid, she declared that all her objections to God's Providence had faded away. Three times she asked her friend to say the Lord's Prayer with her.

6

Forty-six Years of Hidden Life
(1831–1876)

FROM February 5, 1831, when Catherine went to the Hospice d'Enghien, until December 31, 1876, the time of her death there, nothing that would attract attention happened in her life. The novice who had been favored with visits from the Blessed Virgin and who had twice seen her guardian angel walking by her side, now led an existence monotonous and obscure, and this for a period of forty-six years. It was in this way that she was to sanctify herself and to fulfill the world-wide mission with which God had charged her.

She rose daily at four, while the old men to whom she ministered were still sleeping; she worked in the large garden which lay between the hospice and the Maison d'Oeuvres. Here she would pause briefly to pray before the statue of Our Lady on her way to the chapel of Reuilly where the two communities held their religious exercises together. Even when she became old and lame, she was always among the earliest arrivals. Austere and sturdy, she did not avail herself of the authorization given to Sisters who wished to take some extra hours of sleep on a certain day each week.

During the hour of adoration that preceded Mass, she remained on her knees motionless, the tips of her fingers on the elbow rest, her eyes fixed either on the tabernacle or the figure of Our Lady. At five-thirty Mass began and, on the days when the Rule allowed it, Catherine would receive Holy Communion. She gave much thought beforehand to her Communions. She would sometimes say to the younger Sisters who needed encouragement: "Come, my dears, you must make yourselves ready for tomorrow's Communion, by offering today some sacrifice to God."

After breakfast she began the long day's work. As we have said, during the first five years she was attached to the kitchen and the laundry. It was her duty to prepare the plates of food that were to be carried to the various guests of the house. Putting aside the finest portion she would say respectfully: "This is for Sister Superior." Whatever seemed most attractive was served to those who were ill; when all these had been attended to she would say: "Here is something for the rest of us." Then, as she put aside whatever scraps remained: "This will be for me, if you please."

The Poultry Yard and Gate

After 1836, when Catherine was given the task of caring for the old men, she was also put in charge of the "poultry yard" of the two establishments and made gatekeeper or portress of the hospice as well. There were also cows to be taken care of in this "poultry yard," and it was she who milked them. Her long experience at Fain-les-Moutiers was of value in caring for the setting hens, for the pigeons and for the rabbits. One of the other Sisters who had no farming experience before she came to the convent was responsible one day for the death of a sick pigeon which she had allowed to escape from the dovecote. Catherine was frightfully upset by this, and she explained in detail to her coworker how her negligence was the cause of the young pigeon's death.

For almost half a century Lazarists and Daughters of Charity were asking themselves which of the novices in the seminary it could have been to whom the Blessed Virgin had appeared, and the name of Catherine was sometimes brought up. One day as she was walking in the garden, one of the young Sisters of Reuilly was there with her parents and pointed to Catherine as having been the novice in question. At once, the girl's father went over to Catherine and attempted to pay his respects to "her who had been given the honor of revealing the Miraculous Medal to the world." Catherine bowed her head wordlessly and went off with a shrug of her shoulders as though she did not know what it was all about. After her parents had gone, the young girl came to apologize.

"Why do you take it on yourself to tell such stories?" asked Catherine.

"In the seminary someone told me that it was the Sister who is in charge of the poultry yard at Reuilly who had seen the Blessed Virgin."

"Ah well, my child, it is not always wise to believe all that one hears, and for the future you will do better if you do not talk so much at random."

This tale shows both that it was customary in the congregation to speak of her in connection with her least exalted duties, and also that she made use of brusque retorts in order to preserve her great secret.

The Portress

In 1875, the year before her death, Catherine had grown so infirm that she did no more than say her rosary and attend to her duties as portress.

Monseigneur Fages, secretary to the Archbishop of
Paris, Cardinal Richard, came to her one day on the pretext of having some business at the hospice. Actually, however, his purpose was to sound Catherine on the subject
of the apparitions. He himself has said that the conversation started off very well, but as soon as he began
to phrase his questions more definitely, the old portress
returned him such "short answers" that he went back to
the archbishop's office no wiser than he had been when
he had set out for the hospice.

Nevertheless, visitors for other purposes had no reason
to complain that they were received ungraciously. In
Catherine's eyes all were received as having been sent by
Christ.

The gate was normally closed. On free days she opened
it to all the old men who were going out, wishing them
a good time on their walk, urging them to be careful of
themselves and to keep sober. She reopened the gate
when they returned. If some late comer arrived with un-
steady gait because he had too generously slaked his thirst,
she received him sadly and helped put him to bed. She
waited for the morrow before meting out the needed lesson. She punished with justice and kindness, fitting punishment to the offense. The most serious penalty that she
ever gave — and this was rare — was to require the of-
fender to keep to his bed for three days.

She loved these old men, and she was devoted unstint-
ingly to their service, giving them all the thoughtful care
that a well-bred daughter accords to an aged father. In
winter time, she saw to it that they were warmly clad,
and all the year round that their clothing was clean and
in good repair. When she served them in the refectory,
she would ask if their portions were sufficiently large; and

if this were not so, she would go back to the kitchen to find something else. "My dear, what must be, must be!" she would say to the Sister cook who sometimes expressed amazement at such appetites in men who did no work.

And the old men loved her as well. Her combination of firmness and kindness in her treatment of them brought results. She was deeply grieved by their faults as she regarded these as offenses against God, but even as she scolded, she forgave. When she was reproached for not being more severe, she said: "What can I do? I see Our Lord in them, and it is too much for me."

One of the men claimed to be an atheist, and he behaved in such fashion as to be nicknamed "the Devil." "How wicked your Devil is," said another Sister one day to Catherine, according to a witness at the beatification process. "Tears came to Catherine's eyes, and she answered: 'Well then, if you think him so bad, pray for him.' " She did so herself, and when he came to die, he died like the others, wearing the Miraculous Medal around his neck, and having received the Sacraments. "For the space of the sixteen years in which I was her superior," said Sœur Dufès at the same inquiry, "not one of the old men in her charge died without having been reconciled to God."

In the women's section of the hospice there was a poor old victim of melancholia called *La Noire* (the Gloomy One) because of her depressed spirits. No one was able to do anything with her, and she was therefore given to Catherine as an assistant. Catherine was kindness itself to her, being always patient, calm and tireless in her attention to her needs. When the poor creature went on a hunger strike, it was Catherine alone who could prevail upon her to eat.

Catherine and Her Superiors

It was the wish of St. Vincent de Paul that his religious might be drawn from the "good country girls" of his day. These, he said, are "simple creatures, humble, content with what God gives them, moderate in their use of food and drink as well as being able for hard work." He added that these "good country girls obey without grumbling, seeing in all things the will of God, and being as supple and manageable as is a horse by his rider." All who saw Catherine at work agreed that she fully realized this ideal of "a true Daughter of Charity."

After having received from God at the opening of her religious life the great favors which were given her, she "was content" with what He gave her afterward, although it was no more than a door to open and shut, a poultry yard to keep, and two dozen old men to whom she was obliged to render every conceivable care. "In the last year of her life," one Sister tells us, "I went with some youngsters on St. Catherine's Day to felicitate her on her feast. We found her bent over the fountain in the courtyard, cleaning the chamber pots of the sick.

" 'What you see me doing, my children,' she said, 'is the work of a Daughter of Charity. We treasure this work and we must not allow anyone else to deprive us of it.' "

Of all the obligations of the religious life, one of the most difficult is to see God in religious superiors who sometimes are far from mirroring divine wisdom and kindness. "I have never heard Catherine even discuss, much less criticize, an order," said a Sister who knew her very well. "Should it be that an order went against her grain, her naturally pale face might flush for an instant, but she would not let a word escape her, and she would obey at once."

To young religious she would say: "My children, do not murmur against your superiors, for they are really God's representatives." As she had for long been their senior, she had practically directed the work of her six companions at the hospice; but in 1872, it was decided to name an official "assistant" in charge. All hoped that the title would be given to Catherine. On the contrary, a young religious, Sœur Angélique, was appointed. The little community was prepared to receive her very coldly, but Catherine stole a march on them. She led them to the superior, Sœur Dufès, and spoke in the name of all: "Please be sure that it is enough that authority has spoken. Sœur Angélique will be received among us as one sent by the Lord. We shall obey her as we would yourself." Her companions wished that Catherine might at least remain the custodian of the keys of the house, but she brought them to Sœur Angélique on the very first night.

Summing up the testimony that was brought out at the inquiries, the saint's best historian, Lucien Misermont, has thus expressed himself on the subject of Sœur Dufès, who was Catherine's superior during the last sixteen years of her life: "God has permitted that certain saints have been misunderstood by their superiors, allowing these to use them harshly. If this was not exactly the case with Catherine, it is nevertheless true that Sœur Dufès has confessed that she had never felt drawn to make much of Catherine, . . . but that she felt it her duty to give her opportunities to practice the virtues; she readily made cutting observations of a kind that were painful even when Catherine had not been at all at fault."[1]

When stripped of its euphemisms and its reticence, this brief passage tells a good deal. One trembles at the

[1] Lucien Misermont, *La bienheureuse Catherine Labouré;* 3rd éd. (Paris, 1933), p. 198.

thought of all that a woman who had another under her
control for sixteen years might think of in the way of
exactions, serious as well as petty, once she had taken it
into her head to make the subject "practice the virtues."
Nor are the following lines less telling: "Never have I
known Catherine to disobey," declared Sœur Dufès at
the inquiry, "even in the most trifling matters. If any
sign of dissatisfaction were voiced in her hearing, she
would say simply but firmly: 'One must obey just because Sister Superior has ordered it.' "

Catherine and Her Sisters in Religion

Catherine was always present at the community recreation periods, although her work sometimes made her a
late arrival. She would seat herself in a corner, devoting
herself to her knitting and leaving talk to the others. As
she advanced in age she followed the conventual custom
of taking a seat closer to that of the superior, but she
did not become more talkative. According to the testimony at the inquiries she did not often intervene in the
conversation.

One of the Sisters once declared that the novice to
whom Our Lady showed herself in the Rue du Bac had
not actually seen Mary in person, but a mere image of her.

"I beg your pardon, my dear," said Catherine, "she
saw her in flesh and blood, just as I now see you." Then,
bowing her head, she silently returned to her knitting.

On another occasion, some Sisters stated that those to
whom the Miraculous Medal and the scapular of the Pas-
sion had been revealed had become the superiors of their
communities. "Not a bit of it," replied Catherine. "They

were then, and will always remain, in obscurity; it is needful that they lead a hidden life."

After she had once defended her ideas against those
of another Sister who had contradicted her, the superior
observed: "I see that when the time comes you can hold
to your own opinion."

Catherine at once fell upon her knees to ask pardon,
and she added, "I know very well that I am full of pride."
She was already aged, and the sight of her sincere humility
brought tears to the eyes of many of the Sisters present.

According to the records of the beatification and canon-
ization inquiries, "she was very often treated as if she
were an incapable fool" by companions who happened to
be better educated and better connected but who nevertheless were not really superior to her. She bore all this
with a smile.

"On the few occasions on which she did speak, she accepted the affront in silence if no one wished to converse
with her or even if they did so in mockery. To any
sympathetic soul who might attempt later to offer her
solace she would merely say: "One must see God in
everyone."

There was at one time some consideration given to the
idea of putting Catherine in charge of one of the minor
houses of the congregation, and Mère Devos, who was
then the superior general, called her to the Rue du Bac
for a conference.

"But, Mother," expostulated Catherine, "how could
such a notion ever enter your head? Are you not first
among those who know me to be incompetent?"

Was it her inability to spell that weighed the scales
with the superior general? At any rate, Catherine was

sent back that day to her poultry yard and her old men, and it was with joy in her heart that she returned to them.

Catherine and Her Family

The incident of the promotion which was not made was told by Catherine to her nephew, M. Meugniot, the son of Tonine. She had married at Viserney, not far from Fain-les-Moutiers, and had had several children. M. Meugniot was the object of special interest on the part of "Aunt Zoé," as Catherine continued to be known in the family. When he was twelve, she had obtained his admission to the Lazarists' College at Montdidier. After he reached the age of seventeen she sent for him to visit her at Enghien, and asked if he had made up his mind to be a priest.

"Should you wish to join the priests of Saint-Lazare, I can have you received by them," she told him. "It is an interesting life: you might become superior, you might also travel, seeing foreign lands, go on the missions, even be sent to China to shed your blood as was the case with the venerable Père Perboyre."[2]

"While she was speaking," says M. Meugniot, "she held in her hands a reliquary containing some pieces of the martyr's vestments. I wondered whether she were not making fun of me; and in leaving I asked to have more time to think things out. Later, I understood that she was seeking to learn whether I was being guided by supernatural motives in my choice of a vocation." As a matter of fact, Catherine's prophecies were fulfilled, for after becoming a Lazarist M. Meugniot traveled widely, served

[2] A Lazarist priest beatified by Pius XII.

as a missionary in China, and was several times a superior in his congregation.

Catherine kept all her love for her family. She was much concerned about one of her brothers who had abandoned the practice of religion, and she sought assurance that he might not die without the Sacraments. She helped another brother on his deathbed, and we have already recorded what she did for Marie-Louise when she left her convent, and then finally re-entered it.

After becoming a widow, Catherine's other sister, Marie-Antoinette, the sweet Tonine of Fain-les-Moutiers, took up her residence in Paris. This led to a revival of the affectionate ties that bound the two sisters. Tonine had suffered much in her lifetime, and one day she said to Catherine:

"Had I foreseen what has happened to me, I would have become a religious like you."

"Don't talk in that fashion," said Catherine. "Each of us follows his own calling. Had you done as I, you would not have been able to give one of your sons to God."

On January 18, 1874, Tonine, who had been confined to bed for a long time, went into a coma and was unable to speak or to recognize anyone. Catherine came to see her at about one in the afternoon. She asked her niece, Madame Duhamel, to leave her alone with the dying woman. What occurred between them? . . . She remained for almost an hour alone with her sister. Then she came quietly out of the room and said to her niece: "Go in now, to see your mother." Tonine had regained her senses; she was able to express her last wishes to her daughter, then she relapsed into the coma and died quietly on the following day at about eight in the morning.

Prophecies

Was Catherine favored with the gift of prophecy? Some ten predictions are attributed to her and all, save two, have been fulfilled. Among those which have been recognized as having come to pass, we may note the following:

A great fire having started in a paper mill near the Reuilly house of the Daughters of Charity, the Sisters were fearful lest the flames would spread to their buildings. Catherine remained quite calm, and seemed entirely unmoved by the common excitement. She went about her usual tasks, and she said only that all the fuss would amount to nothing. This proved to be the case.

One day in 1875 the bell rang. It was the Abbé Olmer, a chaplain of the diocese of Paris who, from time to time, came to visit the hospice.

"Good morning, M. le Curé," said Catherine as she opened the door.

"Ah, Sister, since you call me 'curé' evidently you do not recognize me."

"I recognize you perfectly; but curé is what you soon shall be, in a parish dedicated to the Immaculate Conception of Our Lady."

All this concerned a new parish being founded in the district to which the archbishop had already given the name of Sainte-Radegonde. However, he was soon to change his mind: the parish was dedicated to Mary Immaculate and the Abbé Olmer became its pastor.

Neither old men nor old women at the Hospice d'Enghien were required to don any special kind of dress; there seemed to be no necessity for such a requirement, nor had there ever arisen any question of them being transferred elsewhere. Therefore it afforded Catherine's companions an opportunity to mock at her when she one day declared to them: "I have seen all our old people garbed in uniforms, the men dressed in blue, while the women were in black. They were living in a great château on the side of the river, and over the château I read these words: 'Hospice d'Enghien et d'Orléans.' " Catherine had been already dead for a quarter of a century when, on May 1, 1901, the old people of Paris went on a journey into Touraine in order to take up their abode in the old Château d'Amboise on the Loire. They have since worn the uniform in which Catherine saw them, and over the gate of their new home one may read: "Hospice d'Enghien et d'Orléans." The addition was made in deference to that princely family — the house of the Duc d'Orléans — which supported the institution after the line of Enghien had become extinct.

M. Aladel had published, within the space of a few years, eight editions of *La Médaille Miraculeuse*; but in 1842 his penitent told him that, as far as she was concerned, she would not even see any more. And, as a matter of fact, the ninth edition of the booklet did not come out until 1878, two years after Catherine had died.

She foretold her own death long months in advance of it; and she added that there would be no need of a hearse to take her to the burial place. As we shall see, this was verified in a fashion quite unanticipated.

About 1833, she had said to her confessor: "M. Aladel, the Blessed Virgin wishes you to carry out yet another mission. You are to found and direct a confraternity of the Children of Mary; the Blessed Virgin will shower many graces upon the members of this confraternity; indulgences will be granted them; and there will be many feasts to be celebrated."

Up to that time this type of confraternity did not exist except in Rome, in a small orphanage in Paris, and in the colleges of the Jesuits and of the Ladies of the Sacred Heart. M. Aladel set to work with the help of his fellow Lazarists and with that of the Daughters of Charity. For recruits he sought mainly among young women in the ordinary walks of life. The confraternities that he founded increased and flourished so well that by 1877 they numbered almost twelve hundred, spread throughout the world and including more than 90,000 members. Pope Pius IX and Pope Leo XIII granted indulgences to them, and from that time the month of May began to be celebrated with increased splendor.

The Paris Commune

The most notable among all Catherine's predictions is that which announced the death of Monseigneur Darboy, the archbishop of Paris. But here, as before, the saint confined herself merely to repeating what Our Lady had told her on the night of July 19, 1830. It will be recalled that Mary had then spoken of events which would take place "forty years later."

This space of forty years takes us to the Franco-Prussian War of 1870, which ended in the defeat of France. Then came an attempt of the Communists, or "Communards" as they were then called, to seize power in France. They were successful in the capital only, and that for no more than three months. This is what historians call "the Paris Commune." It lasted from March 18 to May 28 in 1871.

"Indeed there will be great danger," Our Lady had said, "but I shall be with you. . . . St. Vincent will watch also over his two families. . . . It will not be as well, alas, with other religious houses, wherein there will be many victims. There will also be victims among the clergy of Paris. The Archbishop himself will die; the Cross will be insulted. . . ."

It is a fact that neither the Daughters of Charity nor the Lazarists suffered during the Commune. But many were killed among the Dominicans, the Jesuits and the clergy of the diocese. Monseigneur Georges Darboy, Archbishop of Paris, was also murdered. At this time Catherine reminded her confessor of what had earlier been said by the Blessed Virgin, and she herself had a dream which, for the second time in her life, told her precisely what the future had in store.

The Sisters of Reuilly and Enghien harbored more than two hundred sick and wounded. They had already received several visits from the Communards, visits that presaged no good. On an April evening in 1871, Catherine, who was sitting during recreation at the side of Sœur Dufès the superior, suddenly roused herself from her habitual silence and to the general surprise said:

"Last night I had a dream. I dreamed, Mother, that the Blessed Virgin had come here, into the common room, to look for you. As you were not here she went to your office, but she did not find you there either. Then she sat down at your table, and turning toward me she charged me with this message for you: 'You are to say to Sœur Dufès that she may go away in peace, for I shall take care of the house in her absence. She is going south with Sœur Claire, and will return on May 31 at the month's end.' "

No one attached any significance to these words. Catherine herself, fearful as always lest visions be attributed to her, went to the superior on the following day.

"You know, of course," she said to her, "that what I

told you yesterday evening was no more than a dream I had while I slept."

"I must tell you that I have thought no more of it," replied Sœur Dufès.

However, the Communards were now bearing down upon their enemies. On Spy Wednesday, April 7, they turned up at Reuilly to seek two wounded gendarmes being cared for by the Sisters. They refused to yield the men. On Easter Day the rebels were back again, headed by the new mayor of the thirteenth arrondisement. They demanded that Sœur Dufès point out the gendarmes. Her only reply was to say:

"Never!"

A Communard stepped forward before her and menaced her with his saber. She cried out:

"Do not touch me!"

He let the saber fall. Nevertheless, the revolutionary band made a strict search among the sick. One of the gendarmes who was almost well had managed to dress, and he made his escape by way of Enghien. The other had the good fortune not to be discovered as he lay in his bed among the other wounded.

The Communards were infuriated at their disappointing failure to find those they sought, and they resolved to imprison the superior. At once forty nuns made ready to follow her.

The mayor laughingly cried out: "What can I be expected to do with this flock of fluttering swallows? All of you, stay where you are . . . you are not under arrest." Then he turned to Sœur Dufès: "But as for you, you will hear more from me no later than tomorrow."

On the day following Sœur Dufès managed to escape from Paris and to reach Versailles. After a few days, she began to realize that it would not be possible to return to Paris. She therefore decided to seek asylum in Toulouse where she had spent her early years in the religious life. She took Sœur Claire with her and the two set out for the south. Later on she declared that neither in the choice of her destination nor in the selection of her companion had she, in any way, depended on Catherine's dream, for she had quite forgotten it.

In the meantime, the Communards were establishing themselves at Enghien and at Reuilly. Catherine continued to fulfill her duties as portress and to care for the old men in her charge. She had distributed Miraculous Medals to a number of the soldiers, and others asked that they might have them also.

"But, unhappy men, what will you do with them?" she asked. "You have no belief in anything, have you?"

One of the Communard soldiers replied: "That is very true, my dear Sister. We do not believe in much; but your medal has helped others and why should it not do as much for us?"

Among the troops were some women soldiers who were actually more abandoned than the men. One of them behaved so shamefully toward the Sisters that she was brought before the miltary command. Called as a witness, Catherine testified in such a way as to win acquittal for the creature.

On another occasion, it was Catherine herself who stood in the place of the accused, having been brought to the military tribunal between two soldiers. The judges were unable to understand the Burgundian peasant patois in which she spoke to them, and they dismissed the charges, thinking her to be only an old fool.

The Sisters now understood that they would have to

leave. In the house at Reuilly they had to abandon the
ground floor to the soldiers despite the fact that here were
located both chapel and common room. They themselves
were confined to quarters on the second floor. In order
to avoid the danger of its profanation, they had taken
the Blessed Eucharist with them. On the night of April
19, the Communards were drinking, shouting and singing
in the common room. Suddenly a noise was heard of
many chairs being overturned and heavy footsteps tramp-
ing in the direction of the staircase. Were these drunkards
about to come upstairs and thrust themselves into the
Sisters' quarters? The Sisters took the Blessed Sacrament
and began to give Communion to each other as the Christians of the early Church had done. One of them had already begun the prayers of thanksgiving in a loud voice
when there came a rapping at the door and the leader
of the soldiers and his men appeared on the threshold.
He was thoroughly drunk; but nevertheless what he saw
evidently brought him to his senses, for he suddenly became quiet and yielded to better thoughts, for he now
began to make excuses that the men under him had
turned out to be such noisy drunkards. The upshot was
that he himself slept outside the door, declaring, with a
flurry of oaths, that anyone who wished to molest the
holy women would have him to reckon with beforehand.

For the time the Sisters were safe enough; but the situation had become unbearable, and the next day the two
communities of Enghien and Reuilly decided to disperse.
Catherine and a companion went to the Château de Balainvilliers, some leagues from Paris, where friends of the
congregation gave them hospitality. Catherine was among
the last to leave the hospice, and before doing so she went
to pray before the statue of Our Lady in the garden. Be-

cause she feared it might be profanely used, she took the Virgin's crown off in order that she might carry it away with her. As she came out of the hospice, the soldiers searched her luggage and left it strewn all over the ground. Silently she gathered up her simple belongings and the crown, while the bystanders jeered. As the Sisters passed by, some women on the Faubourg-Saint-Antoine reviled them, threatening them with their clenched fists and making the little children they carried in their arms do the same.

After her arrival at Balainvilliers, Catherine wrote an eight-page letter to Sœur Dufès. This letter is, unfortunately, lost. Once more she assured the superior that the houses of Reuilly and Enghien would be protected and that the Sisters would be able to return by the end of May. On May 18, after learning that the Communards had sacked and defiled the Church of Notre-Dame-des-Victoires, she said to her companion: "They have dared to raise their hands against the Blessed Virgin. Now they are surely lost; they have not much time left." As a matter of fact, it was but three days afterward when the regular troops of the French Republic forced the capitulation of Paris. They conquered the city gradually, drowning the Commune in blood, and by May 28 order had been restored.

Sœur Dufès heard of the liberation of Paris and hurriedly departing from Toulouse she appeared at Balainvilliers on May 30 in search of Catherine and her companion. Together they set out the next day and returned to Paris. The buildings, the chapel, the furniture in both houses were intact; the soldiers had refrained from pillage. Nor had they injured the statue in the garden. It was Catherine's first care that the crown be restored to Our

Lady, and as she replaced it on the head of the statue, she said: "I was right when I said, my own dear Mother, that we would return in time to crown you on May 31."

Catherine and the Interior Life

When she was asked how she prayed, Catherine replied: "After I enter the chapel I place myself in the presence of God and I say to him: 'Lord, here am I; give me whatever you wish.' If he gives me something, then I am happy and I thank him. If he does not give me anything, I thank him nonetheless, knowing as I do that I deserve nothing. Then I begin to tell him of all that concerns me, my joys, my thoughts, my distress, and finally, I listen to him."

This is almost all that we know of her intimate relations with God. It is not certain that the two Lazarists who served as her directors — M. Aladel from 1830 to 1865, and M. Chinchon from 1865 until 1876 — it is not certain that they knew any more. At any rate, it is certain that they did not reveal any more.

There have been discovered some notes — apparently notes made from sermons — that Catherine put together during her early retreats. From these one sees that she wishes to take the Blessed Virgin as her exemplar in life: "To take Mary as my model in all that I do, asking myself what Mary has done, and how and why she did it" (March 1838).

She also kept before her the thought that neither Our Lord nor His Mother were exempt from temptation: "I must keep watch if I am not to lose purity; in my temptations . . . I shall have recourse to Mary who is purity itself" (Retreat of 1842).

Without going into detail, she speaks of her disappointments and her sorrows: "To offer myself to God without reservation . . . in the spirit of humility and penance. Should he wish me to be disappointed, I will offer all to him" (Retreat of 1839). "In all my sorrows, I am to go before the Cross, and to lay them all at its foot" (Retreat of 1843).

We do not know all the sufferings that Catherine bore. No more than in the case of Bernadette of Lourdes did the Blessed Virgin promise that Catherine would be happy on earth. One of her companions in religion recalls that "on the 8th of December in some year that I cannot now be sure of, she betook herself to the Rue du Bac for the feast of the Immaculate Conception. I noticed that when she returned that evening she carried her arm in a sling. She had broken her wrist when getting into the vehicle which had brought her home. I said:

" 'The Blessed Virgin has not taken very good care of you.'

"She raised her eyes to heaven and replied: 'What would you have? It is always flowers of this sort which she sends me on her feast days.' "

It was as natural and necessary to her to pray as that she eat and breathe. We are told that "very often she was seen to interrupt her work briefly in order to visit the chapel of the hospice. She would take off her white apron before going in, and then having passed over the doorsill, she would bow deeply before the altar with slow reverence. (Frenchwomen did not at that time genuflect in church.) Her visit to the Blessed Sacrament might be of no more than a few minutes' duration, but when she came out of the chapel her face would be transfigured."

Many of the Sisters who testified during the inquiry

spoke of her devotion to Mary. "I often had the happiness of saying the rosary with her," declared one Sister. "She enunciated the words slowly just as if she were deriving pleasure from each in its order. More than once she would tell us that we were going too fast." Another Sister spoke of Catherine's custom of never passing through the garden without pausing before Our Lady's statue. And another tells us that "the children of the Reuilly orphanage would sometimes hide themselves in order that they might see Catherine at prayer, and that it seemed to them as if she were then speaking to some living person." One day she was seen by one of the Sisters "standing before the statue, with her hands in the form of a cross, and seemingly in ecstasy."

Did she really achieve the ecstatic state? Could she read hearts? Was she able to influence souls physically at a distance from her? All this is mystery — mystery yet to be unveiled — in the life of one who was called by Pius XII when he canonized her, "the saint of silence." Yet the following narrative allows us to lift at least a corner of the veil. It shows, as well, that in her old age Catherine had a friend, a soul whom she had begotten in the religious life, one who loved her and whom she loved. Yet, just as her whole life was dominated by austerity, it seems fitting that the human consolations of this friendship lasted no longer than a few months.

The Vocation of Sœur Lafon

In 1934, Sœur Marie Lafon, a Daughter of Charity who had originally come from Auvergne, and who was then eighty-five years old, told her story to Colette Yver:

"At twenty-two it was my wish to enter the convent.

My mother was dead and my father did not object to my following my vocation. Unfortunately, I did not know what congregation I wished to join. None of them particularly attracted me; perhaps the Daughters of Charity appealed to me even less than did the others. I made up my mind to go on pilgrimage to Notre-Dame-de-Fourvières to obtain enlightenment.

"On March 30, 1872, I left Cantal, in the Auvergne, the village in which I lived, and on the same evening I arrived at Lyon. The next morning I climbed the hill of Fouvières and went to kneel before Our Lady's statue. 'My dear Mother,' I said, 'show me what road I ought to follow. I beg this of you, for you can easily see that I do not know how to find my way.' After I had prayed much, I believe that I heard a voice saying in answer to my query: 'This matter will be settled at Paris.'

"I thought: 'My girl, you are dreaming. Paris, indeed! How would you fare in Paris, a place quite unknown to you?' Ardently, and for a long time, I continued my prayers when suddenly the same voice again made itself heard, but now it spoke more strongly as if the speaker were at my very ear. 'Go to Paris. You should go to Paris.'

"Nevertheless, I devoted the rest of the day to continued prayer. That evening, at about six o'clock, I went back to my hotel, asked for my bill and then took the first train to Paris. I reached there on the following morning toward four o'clock. As I left the station I asked the first person I saw if there was a Sisters' convent in the neighborhood.

"'Yes,' he said, 'the Daughters of Charity are not far away,' and he pointed out the direction of the Rue de Reuilly.

"It was very dark, almost pitch dark, and after much

twisting and turning I lost my way. I finally found myself
in the Rue de Picpus. There I found a policeman whom
I asked if he knew the convent of the Daughters of Charity.

" 'You are right before it, Mademoiselle,' he replied
as he pointed to the Hospice d'Enghien.

"An old Sister was cleaning the windowpanes, and from
within she saw me and the policeman. Even before I rang
she had opened the gate.

" 'Come in, my child,' she said, as though she expected
me.

"She gave me a chair, and then going to the kitchen
she returned with a good breakfast on a tray. I recall that it
was not coffee that she gave me but particularly good
chocolate. I told her my story, and suddenly she interrupted me.

" 'At what time did you hear the voice telling you to
set out for Paris?'

" 'Between nine and ten in the morning; at about half
after nine, I think.'

" 'Ah yes. . . .' She said this in the manner of one to
whom all suddenly becomes clear.

"And it is because of this," continued Sœur Lafon,
"that I have always believed that I owe my vocation to the
distant intervention of Catherine Labouré (she being in
Paris, and I at Lyon). She heard the cry of distress of
one who was all alone and without help, and she prayed
to the Virgin to help her. It is due to her, as well, that I
was not turned away from the door, for had she not intervened again, I should not have been allowed to stay.

"After I was well refreshed with food, she sent me to
Sœur Dufès at Reuilly. She pointed out the way:
'There, at the end of the passage; the door is the first
one to the left,' she said.

"Sœur Dufès, the superior, did not have the manner of one who sets a visitor at ease, and her response to my story was cold. 'Mademoiselle,' she replied when I had finished speaking, 'it is not our custom to receive every young village girl who arrives at Paris in the morning and who has no introductions from parents or priests.'

" 'But, Sister,' I said, although I was taken aback at my own boldness, 'were I an adventuress, surely it is not to a convent that I would come.'

"At this point, Catherine appeared, and although she was ordinarily reserved, she actually ventured to advise the dictatorial superior to put me to the test. She offered to take me with her to the hospice, and her request was granted.

"She was not given to speech, and we said very little to each other. However, we looked at each other, and that was enough. In her deep blue eyes could be read things which can never be spoken. I read there her affection and her encouragement; and no doubt in my own eyes she could discern my daughterly attachment to her as well as my deep gratitude. I helped her in giving the old men their meals; I assisted her in all her work; in fact I followed her about much as a lost dog who has just been adopted by a good master.

"One day, after looking at me even more searchingly than was her wont, she said: 'It is my belief that it is by God's will that you are here, my child.' That was my own belief, as well, and in the seventy-two years in which I have dwelt upon it my belief has remained constant.

"On June 15 I was officially received as a postulant, and I remained at the hospice until September 25 when I entered the seminary at the Rue du Bac as a novice, and so had to leave my benefactress and spiritual mother."

However, before this separation Marie Lafon was the witness of something which seems to tell much of the graces of prayer with which the saint was favored.

"It happened," said Sœur Lafon to Colette Yver, "that our chaplain, who had been away for a few days, unexpectedly returned and announced that he would say Mass that morning at five-thirty; we had not counted on one being said that day. I was in the chapel at Reuilly, and Sœur Dufès said to me: 'Go quickly to tell Sister Catherine that Mass is about to be celebrated.' I hurried off and found her in the chapel at Enghien; she was on her knees, straight as a statue on her prie-dieu, with her head erect and her eyes turned toward the altar with an intensity and an expression I cannot describe.' I came close on my slippered feet and said quietly: 'Sister Catherine! Sister Catherine!' She made not the slightest move, and her eyes never even wavered. After a few more attempts, I gently seized one of her flowing sleeves and said again: 'Sister Catherine! Sister Catherine!' She remained rigid and did not move so much as an inch. She seemed carved in stone and her eyes looked fixedly ahead. . . . Now I thought she must be dead, and I ran off in terror.

"However, I had no sooner reached the garden than I thought: You will be scolded; they will say: 'Stupid cow from the Auvergne, you cannot even take a message.' Retracing my steps, I went back to the chapel and found Catherine as before. Again I seized her sleeve and this time I said: 'Our good Mother Dufès is asking for you.' I had scarcely pronounced the name of our superior when Catherine rose as if she were on a spring, and she began to follow me as quickly as her bad leg would allow. As for myself, I feared now to be late for Mass, and I hurried on ahead. Then I heard her clap her hands and say:

" 'What! will you leave me alone? . . . Please give me your arm.'

"I obeyed. She took my arm and when we came to the statue in the garden, she stopped and began to say an *Ave Maria* very calmly and very slowly. I said to her:

" 'We shall miss Mass.'

" 'Don't feel upset,' she replied, 'we have plenty of time.' And she repeated three times the invocation, 'O Mary conceived without sin . . .'

"And so, in fact, we did, for when we arrived at the chapel, the chaplain was just coming out of the sacristy on his way to the altar to begin the Mass."[3]

[3] Colette Yver, *La vie secrète de Catherine Labouré* (Paris, 1935), pp. 211–21.

7

Death and Glory

ON JANUARY 1, 1876, Catherine said that she would not live beyond the year. She repeated this several times. She was now seventy years old; she had been relieved of the care of the old men, and she walked with the help of a cane. She was usually to be found in her place by the door of which she still had charge. Here she sewed, knitted and recited her rosary.

M. Aladel had been dead for eleven years. On April 25, 1865, he who was always so punctual did not arrive at the Rue du Bac to say Mass. When the Sisters sent word to the Rue de Sèvres, it was discovered that he was in his room lying on the floor. The collar of his soutane was open and his hands, already grown cold, were clutching his breviary.

M. Chinchon became his successor; and it was to him that Catherine henceforth made her confessions and her confidences. It was upon him, too, that she relied for the completion of the part of her mission which was as yet unfulfilled. However, in May 1876, the superiors decided that M. Chinchon should confine himself to directing the novices of the Lazarists only, and M. Chevalier was appointed to replace him as confessor to the Sisters. This change was to Catherine an unexpected blow, and for some days after she was dreadfully upset. She had no more than a few months to live; how could she succeed in this short space of time in prevailing upon the new confessor to do what neither M. Aladel, in thirty-five, nor M. Chinchon, in eleven years, had agreed to do?

She who had sought only to remain unnoticed, she who had never asked for anything, now made bold to request an audience with the superior general of the Lazarists. This was granted, and having presented herself at the Rue de Sèvres, she begged that the general would allow M. Chinchon to remain her special confessor. However, the superior general saw no reason to grant such a favor to the old Sister who had been the keeper of the poultry yard at Enghien, and he sent her away with a few kind words.

When she returned to the hospice, Catherine sobbed out the story of her rejected request to Sœur Dufès. The superior had never seen her cry and was herself very much upset by this grief. For the first time, she seems to have been sympathetically drawn to her unhappy old companion. She tried to comfort her.

"Mother," said Catherine, "I have not much longer to live, and perhaps the time has now come for me to speak. However, since I have been bidden to speak to no one other than my confessor, I can say nothing to you unless I am empowered to do so. Tonight, in my prayer, I will confide the matter to the Blessed Virgin, and will seek permission to speak. Should she grant my request, I will tell you all in the morning. Otherwise, I shall have to keep silent."

Sœur Dufès declared that these mysterious words were the cause of great distress to her; and it was anxiously that she awaited the coming of the next day.

A little before ten the next morning Catherine asked her to come to the parlor of the hospice.

"I thought," she said, "that here you would be less inconvenienced, and that we would find it easier to talk."

They began to talk at once with such absorption in what was said and heard that they did not even take time to sit down. When the midday Angelus sounded, they were still standing. The old Sister had finally revealed the secret which, hitherto, no one but her confessors had shared with her. She told Sœur Dufès that she was the novice to whom, forty-five years before, the Miraculous Medal had been revealed in the seminary. She told of her visions, of the messages she had received, and of the mission which had been entrusted to her.

Sœur Dufès later declared: "How often, as she spoke, how often did I feel like falling at her feet to ask her for-giveness."

Our Lady of the Globe

All that the Mother of God had asked, said Catherine, had been fulfilled, except for one thing which still re-mained in suspense.

"And," she added, "it is this which has turned my life into a martyrdom."

It will be recalled from the description of the two phases of the apparition of the Miraculous Medal (cf. Chapter III) that in the first Our Lady had clasped a golden orb to her breast. This orb symbolized the earth, and it was Mary's wish thus to show how dear this world is to her, and how great is her love for all its people.

"And it is for this reason," said Catherine, "that she has actually asked me, during my prayers, to have a statue made showing her in this fashion, and moreover to have a commemorative altar set up in the place where the appari-tion occurred."

At first Sœur Dufès took this to mean that the image engraved upon the Miraculous Medal was to be changed.

"Not at all," explained Catherine; "the medal is to stay as it is. The medal is one thing; this statue is something quite different."

There was no one at the Rue de Sèvres or at the Rue du Bac to whom the idea of Our Lady and the Globe meant anything at all; nor could anyone recall that M. Aladel had ever mentioned it. Nevertheless, he had done so. Sœur Dufès discovered that there were two elderly Sisters who had acted as his secretaries. She wrote them, and from one, Sœur Grand, who was then in Auvergne, she received this reply:

"Yes, my dear Sœur Dufès, our loving Queen did show herself holding the ball representing the world to her heart, and looking at it with the greatest tenderness. I have even a drawing of this" (June 24, 1876). This drawing, which dated from 1841, had been made that it might serve as a model for a statue which M. Aladel then purposed to have made. Why had he not followed up this project? Sœur Grand did not know. "All that I do know," she added, "is that things went no farther than they were."

Sœur Dufès was both resourceful and energetic. Together with M. Chevalier, she undertook to carry out what they both considered to be an order from the Mother of God. She therefore commissioned a Parisian called Froc-Robert who made statues, to cast a figure of the Virgin of the Globe in conformity with Catherine's directions. When Catherine saw the miniature that the sculptor brought she could not refrain from making a grimace, and she declared: "Actually, it is not bad; but the Holy Virgin is much lovelier looking than that."

The statue was soon completed. But it required more

time to have it placed upon the commemorative altar in the chapel of the Rue du Bac. It took no less than twenty years of persistence on the part of Sœur Dufès and her supporters to bring this about. The project found opposers in both congregations. They feared that the novelty of it would affect the Miraculous Medal adversely; they even went so far as to suggest that Catherine had begun, after her long life, to confuse her own pious desires with the wishes of heaven, and that it would be better to leave things as they were. Nor did discussion and opposition finally die out until 1896, when Pope Leo XIII granted formal approval to the statue of Our Lady of the Globe.

Catherine's Death

As soon as Catherine saw that Sœur Dufès and M. Chevalier had undertaken the project of the statue, she recovered her equanimity; her life ceased to be "a martyrdom"; and, as she herself said, she no longer feared "to appear before the Blessed Virgin."

Her own humility was unchanged, and she said to her superior: "I knew nothing; I was nothing; for this reason, God picked me out." She became as uncommunicative as before on the subject of her vision, and the public remained in ignorance of the name of the Sister who had been so privileged in the Rue du Bac.[1]

On August 18, Tonine's daughter, Madame Duhamel, née Meugniot, came to visit Catherine and brought her

[1] In her book, *La Sœur Nathalie Narischkin*, written in 1876 and published in the following year, Madame Augustus Craven expressed herself as follows: "The humble Sister who was the channel through which there came to us this grace (the grace of the Miraculous Medal) was still living at this time (in 1841); but no one knows even her name." Madame Craven was born a La Ferronays, and was the eldest daughter of the Comte de La Ferronays of whom we have spoken in Chapter 5.

two little daughters with her. "Aunt Zoé," as she was called by her family, gave the older child her "first Communion gift."

"But," said Madame Duhamel, "there is no hurry. The child is but ten years old, and it will be next year before she receives her first Communion."

"Next year," said Catherine, "I shall not be here."

"Come, come, dear Aunt! Why should you not be here? You are no more ill than usual."

"You may believe me or not, as you wish; but I tell you again that I shall not see the year 1877."

From September 8, the feast of Our Lady's Nativity, Catherine was confined to bed. To her knee trouble there was now added some difficulty with the heart and a persistent asthmatic condition. However, she recovered, and in November she was able to follow the annual retreat held at the Rue du Bac.

"This is the last retreat I shall ever make," she said to the Sister sacristan of the motherhouse.

The sacristan took this as a joke, so unlikely did it seem to her. However, she did offer Catherine a cushion upon which to kneel while at chapel, but Catherine refused to make use of it.

After her return to Enghien, she began to show signs of failing; difficulty in breathing became more frequent and more painful. Toward the end of the octave of the Immaculate Conception (December 15) she began again to speak of her speedy departure, saying that the year would come to its close without her, and that there would be no need of a hearse to take her to the cemetery. But no one paid any attention to these remarks.

She was no longer able to carry out her duties as portress, and she was confined to the infirmary at Enghien.

According to the curative practices of the time, leeches were used in order to diminish her sufferings and to help her to breathe more comfortably.

The days immediately preceding her death were in no way more remarkable than any of the other days of her life had been. At about nine in the morning, she would take some bouillon. Later the Sister cook would come to ask what she would like for her noonday luncheon.

Her reply was: "Whatever you wish to give me; whatever you have."

"No more of this. I want you to tell me what you would *like* to have."

"Ah well; bring me a scrambled egg, if you will be so kind."

Of the fifty Sisters at Reuilly and Enghien, the Sister who was appointed as Catherine's nurse did not really know her business; she showed little devotion to her work, and often she seemed to have no time for her patient.

"My dear nurse is not a very hard worker," Catherine once said, speaking, no doubt, to the nurse herself.

This "dear nurse" made quite a scene one day about Catherine not having taken some medicine which had been prescribed; but she actually was mistaken. Catherine, however, allowed her to storm away, and it was only after she had gone that she said to a Sister who was nearby: "You see how she treats me; and this is the first time that she has been near me today."

At the process of beatification the "devil's advocate" brought up this point against Catherine's cause. He also reproached her with having complained of the delay one day before a baked apple was brought to her; and because on another day she had asked for raisins.[2]

2 The "postulator of the Cause" is the official who seeks to bring the

The postulator of the Cause succeeded in showing that this was not a very serious matter. Catherine's remarks on the nurse need not, of necessity, have expressed impatience; they were less complaints than mere statements of what had occurred. Likewise in the matter of the baked apple. The patient had probably wanted to say that it was the same day and not the next day that she wanted an apple brought to her as long as they wished to give her one at all. Who knows if she would be there next day to eat it? As to the raisins, the postulator mentioned three celebrated examples to justify his client; St. Francis of Assisi on his deathbed asked Sister Jacoba, his Roman friend, to make him some of the marzipan that she prepared so well; Thomas Aquinas wanted to eat herring before dying; and Saint Gertrude expressed a desire for fresh grapes.

The postulator also referred to these words of St. Vincent de Paul in the Rule of the Daughters of Charity: "If it should be that any one of the Sisters believes, after she has pondered on the subject in God's sight, that she has need for any special consideration because of the condition of her health, she may suggest this thought directly to the persons who have authority in the matter, and then will peacefully and quietly accept their decision."

Catherine spoke of her death, in the most natural way, as of a journey which she was about to take.

"Have you then no fear of dying?" she was asked.

"Why should I be afraid?" she replied. "Am I not going to be with Our Lord, the Blessed Virgin, and St. Vincent?"

---

beatification process to a successful conclusion. The "devil's advocate" tries, on the other hand, to obstruct it by alleging faults in the character of the servant of God whose life is under investigation, and by striving to establish that the candidate is unworthy of being raised to the altar and given a place in the calendar of saints.

"Before you go, will you not say something to us about the Blessed Virgin?"

"Say your rosary well. Our Lady has been saddened by those in the community who do not do so."

Sœur Dufès wished to entrust to her some messages for heaven.

"I have always been so stupid," said Catherine, "that I do not know how I shall be able to explain myself in heaven. . . . But in the end I hope to be successful; and in that case, Mother, be sure that your commissions will be carried out."

It was to M. Chinchon that she made her last confession.

On the morning of Sunday, December 31, she seemed very weak and it was thought best to administer the Sacraments to her. She received them after she had renewed her religious vows in the presence of the entire community. She was perfectly calm and followed the prayers with attention, responding to them in a low voice.

At about four in the afternoon, she suffered a severe fainting spell. Sœur Dufès was advised of this, and she hurried to her bedside. The patient had recovered consciousness when the superior arrived.

"My dear Sœur Catherine," said Sœur Dufès jokingly, "you forget that this is New Year's Eve and I am very busy; this is not the day on which you should suddenly frighten us."

"They should not have upset you, Mother," replied Catherine; "for the time is not yet quite come."

Madame Duhamel and her two little daughters came to see Catherine. Tonine's daughter tells us: "My aunt seemed very peaceful. She was sitting on her bed, fully dressed, her feet over the side. She gave me a handful of Miraculous Medals, and she gave bonbons to my daughters. She urged them to be always good and devout. She recommended my duties to me, telling me to take care to bring up my children well. When I told her that I should come again on the morrow to wish her a happy New Year, she said to me: 'If you come, you will see me; but I shall see you no more, for I shall have gone.' Noting that she was tired, we embraced her again and left. It was then half-past four."

At about six o'clock, Catherine seemed to be sinking rapidly. The bell was rung and the two communities came to the infirmary. The prayers for the dying, the litanies of Loreto and of the Immaculate Conception were said by her bedside. As Catherine had insistently asked a few days before, the invocation "Mary, terror of the demon, pray for us," was thrice repeated.

"At seven o'clock," according to Sœur Dufès, "without the least pain or any sign of suffering she breathed her last. It was difficult for us to be sure that she was no longer alive."

Glory

Those who were present at Catherine's deathbed did not feel the sorrow which the sight of death usually provokes. One witness declared: "It is a strange thing that when one of our Sisters dies we usually weep and are plunged into sadness; but now we felt no sorrow."

Catherine's body was placed next to the chapel of the hospice on a mound of roses and lilies. Rumor somehow having got around that the old portress of Enghien who had just died was the Sister to whom the apparition of 1830 had been made, people hastened from all sides to see and to venerate her mortal remains. Her face was strikingly beautiful; all her wrinkles had disappeared, and she

seemed white as alabaster. For two days crowds went un-
interruptedly past the bier, touching rosaries and medals
to the dead Sister's habit. Some workmen whose devotion
did not run to carrying either medals or beads with them,
made use of their watches.

These unexpected evidences of devotion inspired the
Sisters with a wish to keep the remains of the Sister who
had seen the visions. They placed her in a triple coffin,
the first being of plain wood, the second of lead and the
third of oak. It was quickly decided that instead of burying
her in the cemetery she ought be laid to rest in the chapel
of Reuilly where there was an unused vault. This sort
of entombment was contrary to the existing police regula-
tions for the city of Paris; but Madame MacMahon, wife
of the President of the Republic, obtained the necessary
permission for this unusual favor. And so it was, that just
as she had foretold, Catherine was not taken to the cemetery in a hearse.

On January 3, at ten o'clock, after Mass had been celebrated in the chapel at Enghien, she was carried by pall-
bearers to the chapel at Reuilly through that garden path
where she had so often walked and so often prayed. Two
hundred and fifty Daughters of Charity formed her escort.
There were, moreover, about ten Lazarists and hundreds
of the residents of the neighborhood in which she had
spent her lifetime. There were no sad faces; a quiet
joy filled all hearts and burst forth suddenly when after
the *Miserere* had been sung, the Children of Mary, seemingly without prearrangement, began to chant the *Ave
Maris Stella* and followed it by a resounding *Magnificat*.
Again they sang when the coffin was lowered into the
vault; this time they intoned a joyful hymn in honor of the
Immaculate Conception. It was as if these young working

girls of Paris could not endure the funereal aspects of the ceremony. It passed their understanding why grief should be felt now that Catherine, she who had seen the Blessed Virgin, who had spoken with her, who had even, as one might say, been enfolded in her arms, had now gone to rejoin the heavenly Mother in Paradise.

Yet neither the Daughters of Charity nor the Lazarists concerned themselves at the beginning with any attempt to secure official recognition of the sanctity of Catherine. They knew that she had always taken good care of the old men who had been given into her charge, that she had recited her prayers well, that she had carefully attended to her duties in the poultry yard and at the house gate, that she had never been the cause of difficulty to her sisters in religion or of concern to her superiors. Yet, as they thought, did an existence so ordinary have anything to recommend that it be held up to the admiration of the Christian world in general?

It was actually a Jesuit, Cardinal Aloisi Masella, prefect of the Congregation of Rites, who induced Catherine's religious family to seek her beatification. His duties had required him to devote some attention, in 1894, to the liturgical feast of the Miraculous Medal, and he was seized with enthusiasm and wrote to one of the Lazarist superiors:

"Sixty-four years have gone by since the Immaculate Virgin was pleased to show herself to Catherine Labouré. The medal which was the chief result of this apparition has been the cause of uncounted miracles throughout the world, one of the greatest of them having taken place in Rome itself and having been subjected to a most strict investigation. Yet, scarcely anything is known of how all this began. . . . The name of this saintly woman, Catherine

Labouré, is scarcely even mentioned. . . . Well, I have at least made certain that it is (recorded) in the Office of the Feast (in the sixth lesson at Matins), in the same way that Bernadette's name is mentioned in the Office of the Lourdes Apparitions."

In 1895 the superior general of the Daughters of Charity called on Cardinal Masella to thank him, and that prelate asked how soon she proposed to introduce the "cause" of Sœur Catherine Labouré. The superior replied that little thought had been given to this.

"What!" exclaimed Cardinal Aloisi-Masella. "Why, here is a religious of outstanding holiness. If you do not take this affair in hand, I shall do so myself."

The family of St. Vincent de Paul then began the procedure destined, after many years, to raise the servant of God to the honors of the altar. So it was that Catherine was beatified on May 28, 1933, by Pope Pius XI, and was canonized by Pope Pius XII, the reigning Pontiff, on July 27, 1947.

On March 21, 1933, the act of recognition and authentication of her relics had taken place in the chapel of Reuilly. Only a few persons were present: Cardinal Verdier, then Archbishop of Paris, two physicians, a police official, the undertakers, some Lazarist priests and some of the Sisters, among whom were two or three who had actually known Catherine.

Her body was found intact. Her hands were joined as though she still prayed. Her white cornette had fallen forward and when it was lifted up her gentle face was seen to be scarcely darkened. One of the doctors lifted her eyelids and suddenly fell back with an astonished exclamation. So, too, did the others who were close to the bier; for the dead Sister seemed to be looking at them with her lovely blue eyes as if she still lived. Her neck, her arms, in fact her entire body, retained its suppleness.

She was then vested in a fresh cornette and robe, and as they were dressing her it seemed as if she were still living. She was laid to rest in a magnificent reliquary and brought back to the Rue du Bac, to the very place where, a century earlier, Mary had commissioned her to give the Miraculous Medal to us.

It is there, under the altar of Our Lady of the Globe, that she now rests; and there she daily receives, in her kindly way, the many pilgrims who come to seek the intercession of our heavenly Mother, and who ask Catherine also to pray for them.

Part Two

OTHER APPARITIONS OF
OUR LADY
IN MODERN TIMES

8

✠

La Salette

(1846)

WHEN set within their historical context, the supernatural manifestations of the Rue du Bac are seen as part of a whole, the first links in a chain, the opening words in a message that was to continue throughout the whole of a century. We would risk either underestimating or exaggerating the significance of these apparitions were we to consider them apart from others that followed and are closely knit with them. Anyone who wishes really to understand them must read the entire message which they introduce, and to do this he must know something of the later apparitions.

It is for this reason that we offer here a summary account of the visions with which the Mother of God has favored seventeen other persons between 1830 and the present time. Thus we may see how they both refer back to and complete the visions which gave birth to the Miraculous Medal; how together they form one integral message; and how this message, given to us by Our Lady in our own time, is in accord with the message of Our Lord revealed to us in the Gospels.

The apparitions at La Salette took place fifteen years after those in the Rue du Bac. La Salette-Fallavaux (Isère,

151

France) numbered then three hundred inhabitants. It is in the Alpine section of Dauphiné, at a level of about six thousand feet, and about forty miles from the Italian frontier.

The two children to whom Our Lady came to speak on September 19, 1846, had been hired as cowherds by local farmers. One, Maximin Giraud, was eleven years old; the other, Mélanie Calvat, was fifteen. They had known each other but two days, spoke only the patois of the region, and were not very bright, particularly Mélanie whose first Communion was delayed for this reason until her seventeenth year.

On the day of which we speak the two little cowherds were watching the animals of their respective employers on the mountainside when, at about half-past three in the afternoon, "the beautiful Lady," as they called her, appeared on one of the "paradises" — heaps of stones in the form of an altar and adorned with flowers — which they had built to pass the time. Mélanie was the first to see her. They hurried to the place called the Little Fountain which she pointed out to them. They first saw a globe of light which opened up, and then a woman sitting on the stones of their "paradise" with her feet in the dry bed of the brook. Her elbows rested on her knees, and her face was hidden in her hands.

Mélanie was so startled that she dropped the stick she was carrying.

"Pick it up," cried Maximin. "If she does anything to us, I will give her a good crack with my stick"; and he brandished the rod he himself carried.

Suddenly the Lady raised herself and folded her arms.

"Come here, my children," she said. "Do not be afraid; I have come to tell you great news."

They came forward and were able to look at her more closely: her bright hair was gathered with a diadem and a wreath of roses; a white kerchief, bordered with roses, covered her shoulders; her dress was of shining white shot with gold. On her breast there hung a crucifix by a chain which was suspended from her neck. Another chain seemed to be weighing down her shoulders, and she wore an apron of gold and white slippers with golden buckles and roses around them.

The lovely face of the Lady expressed deep sorrow. Maximin saw only her brow and chin. Mélanie noted her hair, held in place by a band, and she saw that great tears fell from her eyes. It is for this reason that Our Lady of La Salette is called "the Weeping Virgin."

It was a lengthy message that she gave the two young children, and it is astonishing they remembered it so well. As things turned out, they repeated it hundreds of times without ever making a change.

"If my people do not willingly submit, I shall be forced to allow the arm of my Son to weigh down! For how long a time have I grieved because of you. I have had to pray unceasingly lest my Son abandon you. You can never understand how much sorrow I have known.

"I have given you six days in which to work and have marked the seventh as my own day; but you have not been willing to grant me even this. There are carters who, as they drive, swear continually and use the name of God in vain. These are two things which will draw down my Son's vengeance.

"It will be your own fault should the harvest fail. Last year, I gave you warning by the failure of the potato crop, but you paid no attention. Indeed, when you found the potatoes to be spoiled, all you did was to swear. As a result, they continued to wither, so that by Christmas time there were none."

At this Mélanie turned to Maximin as though to ask what were these "potatoes" (*pommes de terre*).

"Ah, my children," said the Virgin, "you do not understand French very well, do you? Well, I shall speak to you more clearly."

Making use of the local patois, she repeated what she had said, and then continued: "If you have any grain, it will be useless to sow it! All that you sow will be eaten by animals or will fall into dust as you flail it. The walnut crop, too, will fail and rot."

Then the Virgin went on in French. But, although Mélanie saw her lips move, she could no longer hear what she was saying; this was a secret heard by Maximin alone. Then Mélanie was given a message for herself alone and this time it was Maximin who heard nothing.

The beautiful Lady then began again to speak in the local patois: "If sinners will but be converted, the very stone and rocks will be changed into heaps of grain, and the potato fields will be rich and will bear abundantly."

She then questioned the little cowherds: "As for you, my children, do you pray as you should?"

"Not very well, Madame."

"Ah, my children, you should pray each morning and evening. Say at least one *Pater* and one *Ave* whenever you can do no more. But when you have the time, you should say more."

Again she began to reproach the people in general:

"All summer there have been only a few old women at Mass on Sunday; the others work instead. It is only during the winter that they go to Mass when they do not know what else to do. Their behavior is so bad that it is but a mockery of religion. And during Lent, all devour meat like dogs.

"Have you seen the waste grain yet, my children?"

"Oh no, Madame," they replied.

Speaking to Maximin, she reminded him: "Think back, for you have already seen it. Do you remember the time you went with your father to the side of the Terre du Coin? The owner of the farm said to your father: 'Come here and see how my grain is spoiled!' Both of you went forward to see, and your father took a few ears in his hand; he crushed them and they crumbled into dust. A little later, when you had gone on about half a league, your father gave you a piece of bread and said: 'My boy, eat bread this year, for I do not know that you will have any to eat next year if the wheat goes on spoiling this way.'"

"Ah, that is so, Madame," said Maximin. "Now I recall it; but I had forgotten."

The Virgin added in French: "Now, my children, you are to pass on to my people what I have told you."

She crossed the brook, and without turning she said again: "My children, will you not tell all my people what I have told you?"

These were her final words. She went toward the plateau, walking half a foot above the earth without ruffling the tall grass or without bending forward to go up the incline.

The children went with her, Mélanie in front, and Maximin behind her, to the right. When they had come to the top of the ridge, she remained for a moment as if suspended about five feet from the ground; then she raised her eyes to heaven and gradually disappeared.

While her feet could still be seen, Maximin put out his

hand and grasped one of the roses on her slipper; but it dissolved in his fingers. The children were at first speechless after this experience; then they shared their impressions of it.

"It must have been God," said Mélanie, "or the Blessed Virgin of whom my Father speaks, or some great saint."

"Ah," replied Maximin, "if I had thought that, I would have asked her to take us away with her."

The discussions set on foot by the news of this sensational happening were beyond imagining. However, from the beginning, the bishop of Grenoble and the majority of the French episcopate expressed confidence in the reality of the apparition and in the authenticity of the message. For a short time, the Curé of Ars was on the side of the skeptics, but he too later accepted them as true. On countless occasions the little cowherds were urged by the indiscreet to reveal their "secrets" to them; but they consistently refused to speak of this part of the message to anyone but the Pope.

Pius IX did ask to know the secrets, and one day in July 1850, seated at desks in the house of the Archbishop of Lyon, the two who had seen Our Lady wrote letters to be delivered to Rome. Four witnesses were present.

Mélanie, who was then nineteen years old, asked to know the meaning of the word "infallible." She was told that the sense of the word depended on its context. "Will come about infallibly," she then said in elucidation. A little later she asked the meaning of "defiled." She was given the same answer and then she explained that she wished to write "defiled city." Her last question was how to spell "Antichrist."

Maximin wished to know the spelling of the word "pontiff." His letter was divided into two paragraphs which he had numbered. All that is known of the letter is the beginning: "Most Holy Father, on September 19, 1846, a Lady appeared to me. It is said that she was the Blessed Virgin. You shall judge of this by what follows."

When the Pope received these letters and had begun to read them, "he set his lips together tightly and puffed out his cheeks" as if to repress some strong feeling. When he had finished, he said: "These letters show the candor and directness of these children." Then he added: "France is menaced by all these perils. But it is not that country alone that is guilty. Germany, Italy, all of Europe, deserve punishment. As for myself, I have less to fear from open impiety than from indifference and human respect. Not without reason is the Church called militant; and in me you see her leader." Beyond this, Pius IX always showed his approval of the occurrence at La Salette.

On November 4, 1874, a poor man of forty who was soon to be carried off by death dragged himself to the place of the apparition. He was one of those rolling stones that gather no moss. This solitary pilgrim had traversed much ground, without ever establishing himself in any settled way of life. Always unstable and improvident, he was yet both honest and virtuous. He had tried to enter the priesthood but had failed; he had studied medicine without succeeding in becoming a physician; he had attempted to settle in twenty other callings without avail. Nine years before this time he had enlisted in the Papal Zouaves; another time he had sought work in Paris and had found only wretchedness. Men had ever been ready to sit in judgment on Maximin Giraud and to condemn him; for wherever he went, he became a focal point of public attention. His greatest fault was that he drank immoderately; but, after all, that is not an un-pardonable fault, and indeed one for which not only Noah but many another has been forgiven.

Now he heard Mass in the beautiful basilica which the priests had built at his direction. He received Communion with great devotion, and then went to drink from the brook, once dry but where water had never failed to flow since the day the Blessed Virgin set foot in its bed. He walked again where as a child he had followed the beautiful Lady who "glided along without bending the grass." Again he told his story in the presence of the Sisters who gave him a night's hospitality. Then casting one last glance at the hill from which the Lady's shining figure had remounted to the skies, he sadly and brokenly went down to the plain again.

The following spring he died. He had received the Sacraments, and he had made this little will: "In the name of the Father, the Son and the Holy Spirit. I believe in all that Holy Church teaches and in all the dogmas that our holy Father the Pope has defined. I believe firmly in, and will defend to the last drop of my blood, the celebrated appearance of the Most Blessed Virgin on the mountain of La Salette, on September 19, 1846, an apparition to which I have testified by my words, in writing and by suffering. After my death let no one say that he has ever heard me deny this great happening, the Apparition of La Salette; for anyone who says this will be a liar."

Mélanie's life was longer and even more sorrowful. She too was a wanderer over the earth, often scorned and sometimes calumniated.

As a young girl she was a Carmelite nun in Darlington in England; later we find her in a convent at Marseilles.

Finally, dispensed from her vows, she lived for years at Castellammare near Naples. Her secret seems to have turned her life upside down. There was a time when it seemed that she could not restrain herself from scratching out the name of Paris from maps or books whenever she came upon it. There is still shown a desk where, while a pupil in the convent at Corenc, she had carved with a knife the words: *Prussians, 1870* — years prior to the Franco-Prussian War.

In 1879 she published her famous secret with the imprimatur of the Bishop of Castellammare. Some prelates asked Rome to condemn the book, for in it harsh reproaches against certain ecclesiastics appeared. All that they were able to secure, however, was a letter from Monseigneur Caterini to the bishop of Troyes in which the secretary of the Holy Office recommended that the work ought not be put into public circulation; but he added that "it may well be read by the clergy; for it will do them much good." Again, in 1916, a Roman decree forbade the "secret of La Salette to be given to the world without authorization."

Mélanie, who had been poor and obscure all her life, died at Altamura in Italy on December 14, 1904. Monseigneur Cochina, the bishop of that diocese, presided at her funeral.

9

Lourdes
(1858)

On Thursday, February 11, 1858, at about half after noon, three poor children of Lourdes went to seek wood along the banks of the river Gave. They were Bernadette Soubirous, her sister Marie, and Jeanne Abadie. They had to cross a mill race where there was a slight flow of water, and Marie and Jeanne who wore only wooden shoes over their bare feet were quick to wade through it. However, the fourteen-year-old Bernadette was a delicate child, and her mother had insisted that she wear stockings because she suffered from asthma. She had sat down to take off her stockings when suddenly a burst of rushing wind caused her to raise her head. She noted with surprise that none of the trees showed any sign of motion. "I must be mistaken," she thought. However, once again the sound of wind struck her ears. Seized with fright, she stood up and looked around. All seemed quiet, except that on the opposite side of the pond she saw the mad quivering of a sweetbriar bush which grew in the crevice of the rocks. Then, all at once, Bernadette noted a brilliance in the niche; it seemed as if lighted by a golden cloud; and a woman appeared within.

"She was young and fair," said Bernadette, "more beautiful than anyone I had ever seen. She looked at me and she smiled. She made me a sign to come forward without fear. And, as a matter of fact, I was no longer afraid; but it seemed as if I no longer knew where I was."

Instinctively, the child reached for her rosary and sank to her knees. "The Lady let me pray alone. It is true she passed the beads of her rosary through her fingers, but she said nothing. It was only at the end of each decade that she joined me in the *Gloria Patri.*"

After the rosary was finished, the Lady stepped back into the rock and the golden cloud vanished.

At first Jeanne and Marie did not miss their companion but when they did, they returned to look for her. Finding her on her knees, they told her that she had been sent there to gather firewood and not to say her prayers.

As they were on their way home, Bernadette who, like her companions, was bowed under a load of wood, asked them:

"Did you see anything strange in the grotto?"

"No, of course not. Why do you ask?"

"Oh, it's no matter."

For the time, Bernadette hugged her secret to herself. But she was not able to keep from speaking about it to her sister Marie later on. And, when during night prayers she broke into sobs and her mother questioned her, it was Marie who hastily revealed what her sister had told. Their parents made fun of the affair and forbade the child to go again to Massabielle.

Regardless of what it cost her, Bernadette obeyed. But on Sunday the fourteenth her companions succeeded in obtaining a release from the prohibition. "Let her go," thought her mother; "she will see that there is nothing there, and so she will be cured of her folly." Doubtless, she must also have said something about the devil, for one of the little girls who went along took some holy water with her.

"There she is! There she is!" cried out Bernadette as soon as they were before the shrub of sweet briar.

"Quickly, sprinkle this holy water on her."

Bernadette did so. "That does not displease her at all," she said. "On the contrary, she has nodded her head and smiled."

Then she fell into an ecstasy in which she remained until they led her into a house nearby. The mother of the Soubirous children arrived in due course, a switch in her hand. "You are a bad lot," she exclaimed, "and you want to make us the laughingstock of everybody who knows us. I will teach you to forget your pious airs and your tales of the Lady." And it was only with difficulty that the bystanders were able to prevail upon the mother not to carry out her threats.

On February 18, at the request of two ladies in Lourdes, Bernadette was allowed to go again to the grotto. This was in the morning. When Our Lady appeared, the child held out to her a sheet of paper, asking that she write her wishes down. This was an idea of the ladies, but it did not appeal to the Lady of the apparition.

"It is not necessary," she declared, "for me to write down what I have to tell you. Promise me that you will return here for the next fifteen days. For my part, I promise to make you happy, if not in this world at least in the next."

On this day, Bernadette did not experience the state of ecstasy, but on February 19, 20, and 21 the witnesses beheld her rapt outside herself during the entire time of the heavenly visitation. A skeptical physician, Dr. Dozous, was present on the twenty-first; after the ecstasy he questioned the child.

She said: "The Lady stopped looking at me for a moment and turned her gaze far from me and above my head. Then she looked at me again and when I asked her why she was sad, she said to me: 'Pray for poor sinners, pray for the world which is so disturbed.' I was at once reassured by the expression of kindness and peace that I saw on her face. Soon afterward, she disappeared."

At this point, we find new entrants upon the scene: the mayor, the imperial procurator, and the commissioner of police. These three came to keep the public order and to preserve the peace. On the morning of February 21 they summoned the little girl who, in their view, was upsetting the village. M. Dutour, the procurator, looked at her severely and said:

"Will you promise me not to go to Massabielle any more?"

"Monsieur, I will not make such a promise."

"Is that your final word?"

"Yes, Monsieur."

"Then be off! . . . We will think this matter over."

In the evening, it was the commissioner of police who called Bernadette to his office. He also pressed her not to go to the grotto again.

"Monsieur," she said simply, "I have promised the Lady that I will return."

"If you do not immediately promise me that you will not go to Massabielle again, I will send for the officers to have you taken to prison."

As a matter of fact, two policemen were stationed at the grotto when Bernardette went there on the following day. Our Lady did not appear, and some wits declared:

"She is afraid of the police; she will show herself no more."
However, she did appear on the following day for the
seventh time. Bernadette was surrounded by two hundred persons. The writer Estrade, who was among them
and who had up until then made a parade of his disbelief,
has described the scene for us:

"Bernadette fell on her knees. As she slipped the first
beads of her rosary through her fingers she fixed a questioning look upon the rock expressing impatient watchful-
ness. Suddenly, as though she had been struck by a flash
of lightning, she shook with wonder; her eyes sparkled
and gleamed; seraphic smiles came to her lips; her whole
being seemed transformed by a grace impossible to describe. Bernadette was no longer Bernadette.

"Spontaneously and in unanimity of movement, all the
men who were present uncovered themselves and bowed.

"After the first transports, Bernadette's attitude became
that of one who listens. Soon afterward, her face and her
motions indicated that she was taking part in a conversation. Bernadette seemed at times to be nodding her head
in agreement; at other times, it was she who seemed to
be asking questions. Whenever the Lady was speaking, she
trembled with happiness; when, on the other hand, she
was expressing her own requests, she bent in humility and
seemed moved to tears. At times it could be observed that
the conversation had been interrupted; then the child
would return to her rosary, but her eyes remained fixed
on the rock. It seemed that she feared to lower her eyelids lest she lose sight of the object of her contemplation.

"This ecstasy lasted for about an hour. Toward its end,
Bernadette moved forward on her knees from the place
where she had prayed to another beneath the sweetbriar
bush that hung from the rock. Here she paused, kissed

the ground, and then, still on her knees, went back to the
place she had left. Her face shone with a final glow of
brightness, then gradually and gently the brightness faded
and disappeared. Before us was nothing more impressive
than the face, pleasant indeed but quite rustic, of the
Soubirous' little daughter. She told us:

" 'While I was praying the Lady said to me: "Go and
drink and wash yourself at the fountain." As I saw no
fountain, I went toward the Gave. The Lady called me
back and made a sign with her finger that I was to go inside
the grotto to the left. I obeyed, but still I saw no water.
Not knowing where to find it, I scraped the earth until
it came. I let it clear itself a bit, and then I drank it and
washed myself.' "

The few drops of water continued to increase all day;
on the following day the flow had grown to the size of a
finger; a week later it was as big as a child's arm. It was
to become a powerful stream, and today is controlled by
many taps and yet yields 32,000 gallons every twenty-four
hours.

Each day, until March 4, Bernadette came back to the
grotto in fulfillment of her promise, and the Virgin met
her there every day except on March 3. (On February 26
she had told the child to "go and say to the priests that they
must build a chapel here.") Then the Virgin showed
herself no more until March 25. On that day, the feast of
the Annunciation, the Blessed Virgin was already in the
grotto when Bernadette arrived. Throwing herself upon
her knees, the child prayed for a long time, then the idea
came to her to ask the Lady to tell her who she was.

At first the Lady smiled and said nothing; but after
Bernadette had humbly repeated her question a second
and a third time, she replied. "At my third request,"

Bernadette tells us, "the Lady joined her hands and raised them to the level of her breast. . . . She looked up to heaven. . . . Then slowly separating her hands she leaned toward me and said: '*I am the Immaculate Conception.*'"

After this, except on April 7 and July 16, the Virgin did not again appear. All in all, she had shown herself eighteen times, at times keeping silence but at others speaking to the child in the dialect of the district.

What followed is known all over the world. And what has taken place at Lourdes during the course of a century is also known. With the exception perhaps of Fatima, there is no place in Christendom which is visited by greater or more enthusiastic crowds of pilgrims.

Until she was nineteen, Bernadette lived at Lourdes with the Sisters of Charity of Nevers. It was while he was visiting their convent one day that the bishop of Nevers, Monseigneur Fourcade, went out into the kitchen where she was paring carrots in order that he might see her. He led her to the parlor and this conversation took place:

"And now, my dear child, what would you like to be?"

"Nothing, Monseigneur."

"Nothing? But one must do something in this world."

"I am with the dear Sisters."

"No doubt; but you are here only temporarily."

"I shall always stay here."

"That will be difficult to do. Just because they have taken you in for the time being as an act of charity, it does not follow that they will keep you."

"Why not?"

"Because you are not a Sister. Now it is true enough that the Sisters of Nevers are allowed to keep servants, but here you are not even a domestic. You cannot hope to continue long in this uncertain status."

Bernadette looked thoughtful and kept silent. The prelate went on:

"You are no longer a child. Perhaps you would like to marry if a suitable person were found?"

Bernadette quickly replied:

"Oh, no; no indeed, as far as that is concerned."

"Well then, why not become a Sister? Have you never thought of it?"

"It is impossible. You know, Monseigneur, that I am poor and that I will never have the dowry required."

"When we find a poor girl with a real vocation, we do not hesitate to receive her without a dowry."

"But," said Bernadette, "the girls you receive without a dowry are trained and educated and can work for you, but I know nothing and am good for nothing."

"You misrepresent your talents," replied the prelate. "I can testify from what I have myself seen that you are good for something."

"For what, Monseigneur?"

"For scraping carrots."

Bernadette laughed and said: "Bah! That is not hard to do."

"That does not matter; one has to know how, and to be willing to do it."

"Monseigneur, I do not yet feel that my mind is made up."

The bishop of Nevers brought the conversation to an end by telling her that if she wished later on to enter the religious life, she need only to write to him.

At first Bernadette said nothing about this conversation; but a year later she went to the superior of the community and told her of her wish to enter the convent. As she fell ill very shortly afterward, she had to wait until 1866 before she was able to carry out her plan.

On the eve of leaving Lourdes, she returned to the grotto where she fell on her knees and began to sob. She kissed the ground several times as she murmured words of love and sorrow. Her heart seemed to be breaking. The Sisters who were with her tried, several times, to lead her away. Each time, she begged to be allowed to stay a little longer. Finally, they succeeded in inducing her to leave.

As they were going back to the convent one of the Sisters said: "Our Lady will hear your prayers at Nevers as well as here."

"Ah yes," she answered, "but in that grotto, I knew heaven."

At the convent of Nevers, where she lived for twelve years, she underwent sufferings of every sort. Those sufferings increased and multiplied. "I am ground like a grain of wheat," she said during her last illness. "Ah! how much one must suffer in order to die!" On Spy Wednesday, April 16, 1878, at about three in the afternoon, she murmured the words of Jesus on the Cross: "I thirst." Then she gave up her soul as she was saying the latter half of the *Ave Maria*: "Holy Mary, Mother of God . . ."

Bernadette has been canonized, and her body, wholly incorrupt, rests in the chapel of the convent of Nevers (Nièvre, France).

10

✤

Pontmain
(1871)

IN JANUARY 1871, at the time of the Franco-Prussian War, there were five hundred inhabitants in Pontmain, a village of Mayenne, situated about two hundred miles west of Paris. The pastor of the village, Abbé Guérin, was a septuagenarian and had occupied his benefice for thirty-five years.

His was an exemplary parish in which many families were accustomed to say the rosary together. The Abbé Guérin himself was particularly devoted to Our Lady. In her honor he had the roof of his church painted in blue sown with stars, and he had placed above the high altar a great statue of the Immaculate Conception; he had established two confraternities, to which almost all his parishioners belonged. When the report of the apparition at La Salette reached Pontmain he had recounted it from his pulpit on the following Sunday, and had concluded his sermon by crying: *"Vive la Sainte Vierge!"* At Pontmain everyone loved and respected Monsieur le Curé.

However, on the afternoon of Sunday, January 15, 1871, the people of Pontmain lacked heart to join in the hymns that ordinarily concluded the Vesper service so great was the sadness that prevailed. It took a special effort on the part of Abbé Guérin to stir them, and he had to say to them several times: "Come, my children, sing your hymn," before they tearfully began to chant "Mother of Hope, we beg your help."

Two days later the anguish was intensified in this poor village which had sent thirty-eight of its sons to do battle with the Prussian invader. Word had now reached Pontmain that the Germans were at the gates of Laval, the departmental capital of Mayenne.

Particular anxiety was felt at the home of the Barbedette family for they had given to the army the eldest of their sons. Snow covered the ground, and the frost was so intense that it seemed as if the stones would crack. In company with his two younger sons, Eugène (twelve years old) and Joseph (ten), the father of the Barbedettes had begun to grind fodder for the horses in his barn at about five-thirty in the afternoon. At five forty-five Jeannette Detais came in. She was known in Pontmain as "the woman who buries everyone," and she was then on her way, as a matter of fact, to prepare a corpse for burial. She brought good news of the elder son of the Barbedettes, the soldier. While the older people conversed, the grinding of the fodder was suspended and Eugène went out to the barn door "merely to see what time it was," as he later declared. Here there took place an apparition of Our Lady which lasted for no less than three hours.

We take our account of this occurrence from a pastoral letter of Monseigneur Wicart, bishop of Laval, who on February 2, 1872, issued his episcopal decision in regard to the marvelous happening.

The prelate begins by setting forth the numerous precautions that he had taken to clear up this matter.

"An inquiry has been in progress since March at Pontmain under the chairmanship of one of our vicars general and with the cooperation of the archpriest of Ernee and the dean of Landivy. During this inquiry both the children themselves and the principal witnesses of all that took place on that memorable evening of January 17 were most carefully questioned. The results of this investigation were recorded in a lengthy report containing both questions and replies, and are now deposited in our diocesan archives. These results appear to be sufficient to establish the reality of the facts alleged; but, in fidelity to our self-imposed rule of proceeding with the utmost caution, we decided to suspend judgement for the time. Some weeks afterward, we ourselves visited Pontmain. On the morning of our arrival the four children had received Communion, two for the first, the others for the second time, while scarcely an hour intervened before they were to receive the gifts of the Holy Ghost in the sacrament of Confirmation. We took advantage of this favorable time to see them, to question them separately, and to consider their replies concerning all that had been said and seen by them on the evening of January 17. We are thus able to affirm that they conducted themselves with perfect calmness and modesty.

"In this way a new and convincing element was added to the facts already in our possession. Nevertheless, some months afterward we determined to open a new inquiry. This second investigation lasted three days during which time the children of Pontmain were subjected to questioning that produced only evidence of their truthfulness, their aversion to lying, and the complete consistency of their replies in respect to the many details they had been able to observe.

"Doubtless, dear brethren, no more than this could be

asked. But another test was added to the two canonical inquiries. A commission of theologians was charged with conducting a most thorough examination of the depositions of the children and of the other witnesses in order to discuss the worth of this testimony, to determine the true character of the facts themselves, in other words, to solve all possible questions that might be raised from the threefold viewpoint of juridical form, philosophical certitude and theological truth."

We now pass to the portion of Monseigneur Wicart's letter that discusses the apparition itself:

"First of all, a boy of twelve, Eugène Barbedette, who came out of the barn in which he was working, then his young brother of ten, Joseph, and somewhat later, two little girls — Françoise Richer, eleven years old, and Jeanne-Marie Lebossé, nine years old — who had joined them without having been told of what had occurred, all alleged that they saw a lady of impressive loveliness standing in the air above the house opposite to where they were. She was wearing a long blue robe ornamented with golden stars, and on her head was a crown of gold.

"Drawn by the joyous and enthusiastic exclamations of the children, the people assembled from every side, and soon more than a third of the population of the little village, with their venerable pastor at their head, were gathered in the place where these wonders were said to be seen.

"Opinion was divided among the watching crowd. Although some believed, the majority were doubtful, or at least they hesitated to place credence in the repeated affirmations of the children. Suddenly, and all at once, while the *Magnificat* was being sung, a long white

streamer was unfurled beneath the feet of the lovely
Lady and on it, traced by an unseen hand, there appeared
in letters of gold the words: "Pray, my children." More
hymns were sung, and to the delighted gaze of the children
new writing appeared. These words they spelled out and
repeated twenty times. As these new letters were added to
those which had preceded them, it was perceived that
they completed the sense of the earlier words by declaring:
'God will soon hear you.'

"The end of the sentence was marked by a period that
glowed like the sun, and it seemed that all was over. But
no, new cries of joy were raised by the children. Again
the unseen hand took up its mysterious work. The inscription was resumed on the line below and completed by
these words: 'My Son has been touched by these prayers.'

"The astonished crowd continued to pray in silence.
However, a voice was raised to intone the hymn 'Mother
of Hope.' Suddenly, the lovely Lady who had been recognized by all to be the Mother of God, raised up her hands
to her shoulders and gently moving her fingers, looked at
the children with a smile of incomparable kindness.

"A little later, when the singers had come to the words:
'My sweet Jesus, now has come the time
To grant thy pardon to our heavy hearts,'
a shadow of sadness passed over the Lady's beautiful face.
In her hands she held up a red cross before her breast,
and upon the cross was the image of Our Lord, also in red.
Above was a white band on which was written the name
of Jesus Christ in red lettering. During this time she
moved her lips and seemed to be praying.

"This was the final phase of the occurrence. For while
the crowd recited their night prayers at the request of the
curé, a kind of white cloth appeared at the Lady's feet

and slowly covered her completely. The crown was seen for a moment by itself, and then in its turn it disappeared. The apparition was over. It had lasted for almost three hours.

"Such, dear brethren," wrote Monseigneur Wicart, "are the essential details."

However, the bishop did not allude to the fact that the vision was also seen by Eugène Friteau, a boy of six and a half; Auguste Avice, four and a half; and a little girl of two and a half who was held in the arms of her mother, the wife of Boitin the village shoemaker. Everyone remarked that the infant extended her arms in the direction of the Virgin, greeting her with exclamations of joy and resisted attempts to turn her away. As for Abbé Guérin, he saw absolutely nothing, nor did anyone else in the crowd, not even the mother of the Barbedette children, despite the fact that she had gone at once to fetch her glasses.

The pastoral letter of the bishop concludes as follows:

"Having reviewed the reports of the two commissions and of the inquiry . . . having reviewed the written testimony of the medical witnesses, having reviewed the report and the recommendations of our theological commission. . . .

"In consideration of the fact that the apparition cannot be accounted for by fraud or imposture, nor put down to an optical illusion or hallucination; considering that the occurrence exceeds the power of man or of any visible and corporeal agency; that it cannot be explained as the result of diabolical forces; that it bears the character of a happening in the supernatural and divine order:

"*Article One*: We judge that the Immaculate Virgin Mary, Mother of God, truly appeared on January 17,

1871, to Eugène Barbedette, to Joseph Barbedette, to Françoise Richer and to Jeanne-Marie Lebossé in the village of Pontmain.

"*Article Two*: We permit liturgical honors to be given in our diocese to the Blessed Virgin Mary under the title of Our Lady of Hope of Pontmain. . . .

"*Article Four*: We have decided on a plan to erect a shrine in honor of Mary on the very spot where she deigned to appear."

As may easily be realized, the apparition caused a great stir. This became all the greater when it was learned that at the very hour she had brought hope to Pontmain, Our Lady seemed to have intervened in military affairs.

As a matter of fact, it was on the evening of the seventeenth that the commander of the German army, General von Schmidt, who had been pursuing the French and was about to enter Laval, received the unexpected order to withdraw. The retreat was begun during the night, and thus the people of western France were spared the vexations of military occupation which they had been awaiting with such fear. This is what is called "the great Miracle of Pontmain." Ten days later a general armistice was signed between France and Germany, and peace was soon to be restored.

Very soon pilgrimages to Pontmain began; they increased in number from year to year. The shrine that Monsigneur Wicart had planned took form as a great Gothic church which was consecrated on May 27, 1877, and later raised by Pius X to the rank of a minor basilica. Hundreds of votive offerings attest both the favors which have been granted to pilgrims and their gratitude for them. From the time when Pius XI, in 1922, granted approval to the liturgical feast of Our Lady of Pontmain, its observance has spread very widely in France, and a great many bishops of that country have inserted it in the "Proper" of their dioceses, so that it is now annually celebrated in a number of places with a special Mass and Office.

The good Abbé Guérin, curé of Pontmain, did not long enjoy the prominence that came to his little parish, for he died on May 29, 1872. As to the children who had seen Our Lady, little Eugène Friteau was already dead a year at the time of the curé's passing; Eugène Barbedette died as curé of Châtillon-sur-Colmont in 1927; his brother Joseph, who had become an Oblate of Mary Immaculate, lived until 1930; Auguste Avice entered the Jesuits and died in 1945 at Shanghai after having spent fifty years as a missionary in China; Jeanne Lebossé joined the Sisters of the Holy Family and died in 1933. The only one to remain in the world was Françoise Richer, who earned a bare existence, sometimes as a domestic servant, sometimes as an assistant teacher in obscure country schools. Toward the end of her life the Abbé Eugène Barbedette offered her a place as servant in the rectory at Châtillon-sur-Colmont, and it was there she died in 1915.

11

Pellevoisin

(1876)

THIS INCIDENT in our chain of events begins with one of those letters such as children in certain parts of Europe write to St. Nicholas. However, here instead of a plea for some mechanical toy, we have a letter addressed to Our Lady by a poor servant girl who felt she was about to die.

"You have not forgotten," she wrote, "that I am your child and that I love you. Restore my poor body to health. Consider the sorrow of my parents. You know very well that they depend wholly on me. May I not finish the work I have begun? If, because of my sins, you cannot grant me a complete cure, at least obtain for me a degree of strength and health that will enable me to earn enough to support myself and my parents. You see, my dear Mother, that they are almost reduced to begging their bread. Think of all that you yourself endured on the night Our Saviour was born, when you were obliged to go from door to door seeking shelter. Think of your suffering when Jesus was nailed to the Cross. I put my trust in you, my good Mother. . . . My family needs me so badly. . . ."

This letter was signed by Estelle Faguette, a servant in the La Rochefoucauld family, employed at their château of Poiriers, near Pellevoisin (Indre), about one hundred and fifty miles to the south of Paris. In the midst of the

177

golden trees of this manorial park is a little grotto like that of Massabielle. Estelle had wished to place her letter, with its request, among the stones that served as a pedestal or throne for the statue of Our Lady of Lourdes; but as she was confined to her bed by her illness, she intrusted this mission to the family governess on a day in the autumn of 1875. Later, we shall see how the Blessed Virgin herself took the trouble to reply to her confident child.

Estelle was then thirty-two; she had been born in the vicinity of Châlons-sur-Marne on September 12, 1845, After her first Communion she went with her parents to Paris, and while still young entered the novitiate of the Augustinian nuns at the Hôtel-Dieu. A serious fall had made her lame, and she was still on crutches when she had to withdraw from the convent. As soon as she was better able to get about she found a position in the family of the Comte de La Rochefoucauld. For twelve years she was valued and loved by her employers, but toward the end of 1875 they were faced with the necessity of parting from her.

It was the concerted opinion of all the physicians who had been consulted that Estelle would very shortly die. She was in the final stages of consumption, and, to say nothing of an abdominal tumor from which she had suffered for a long time, had developed peritonitis as well. Dr. Bucquoy of Paris had pronounced her death to be imminent, and Dr. Bernard of Buzançais had given her up in December.

In January the patient was installed in a little house owned by the La Rochefoucauld family at Pellevoisin, and arrangements were made to have her cared for by the nuns of the village during the final weeks of her life.

Before his departure for Paris, the Comte de La Roche-foucauld had made arrangements through M. Salmon, the curé of the parish, to buy a grave for Estelle in the local cemetery.

On February 10 Estelle asked for Dr. Bernard, but he refused to come, saying that it would be useless, and that he could not take so long a journey just to offer comfort to someone who was certain to die. Dr. Hubert was then called, and as he was a new arrival in the district it was hoped that he might be more willing to please. As a matter of fact, he did put himself out to oblige, but he regretted it at once, for he saw that the poor girl had "no more than a few hours to live."

Thereafter, no other physicians came. It was the Blessed Virgin who visited Estelle, and who, between February 15 and December 8, came fifteen times to see her correspondent of the previous year.

Later, Estelle Faguette was to relate under oath the apparitions and messages with which she had been favored. It is from her account that we can make up a day-by-day narrative of events:

Tuesday, February 15, 1876. This morning, when the curé came to see her, Estelle told him that Our Lady had appeared to her during the night and had said: "Have courage and be patient. . . . You will suffer for another five days. . . . On Saturday you will be either dead or cured. . . . If my Son should grant you life, it is my wish that you make my glory known." The priest thought that his parishioner must be delirious; and, at the stage which she had reached, it did not seem to him as if it much mattered what she said or thought.

Wednesday, February 16. Again, the sick woman said

that Our Lady had been to see her and had said: "Fear not; my Son will grant your prayers. He will restore you to health, and on Saturday you will be cured."

"But my dear Mother, if the choice were mine, I would rather die now that I am well prepared."

"Do not be ungrateful. If my Son restores you to life, it is for your own good. You will not be exempt from suffering; but it is in suffering that merit in life is obtained." In addition to this, Mary confided a secret to Estelle. Again the curé displayed no interest whatever in Estelle's account of all this, for he thought that she had been dreaming.

Thursday, February 17. Again there was an apparition. After she had renewed her promise that Estelle would be cured, Our Lady added: "I am all merciful and I have the key to my Son's heart. . . . What touched me most in the little letter you wrote me in September were the words: 'Consider the sorrow of my parents . . . they are almost reduced to begging their bread.' " The curé now began to waver. In order to be ready for anything he asked the sick woman to repeat all that she had told him before seven other persons. Thus there were eight people at Pellevoisin who knew of the prophecy.

Friday, February 18. Again Our Lady appeared and said: "Have no fear; you are my child, and my Son has been touched by your resignation."

Saturday, February 19. On this morning, the sick woman was completely well. She rose, dressed herself unaided, and ate with good appetite. The tubercular tumor, the peritonitis, the consumption — all were gone, a fact attested to not alone by Dr. Bucquoy of the Académie de Médecine but also by all who, during a space of fifty-three years, up to 1929, saw Estelle Faguette enjoy the best of health. Moreover, even before her cure, the girl had already set before Our Lady her plans for the future: it seemed to her that she should certainly return to the convent. But Our Lady told her that this would not be necessary: "The soul can be saved in whatever walk of life. Where you are, you will be able to do much good and to make my glory known."

July 1, 1876. Again the Blessed Virgin returned; at about ten-thirty in the evening she smiled at Estelle and said: "Be calm, my child; have patience. You will have suffering to bear, but I am with you."

Night of July 2 and 3. This was the seventh appearance of Our Lady. "So great is the love in my Son's heart for me," said Mary, "that he cannot refuse my requests. For my sake he will touch even the most hardened hearts."

Night of July 3 and 4. Doubtless because Estelle was very tired Our Lady said to her maternally: "You are in need of rest and I shall stay with you but a moment." Then she disappeared.

September 9. The vision was seen at about three in the afternoon. "You deprived yourself of my visit on August 15, because you were too upset. You are very French in your wish to know everything without the labor of learning it. For a long time has my Son's treasury been open. If people would only pray!" Then Our Lady lifted up the piece of white wool that she wore on her breast, and Estelle saw that a red heart was imprinted on the material. "The scapular of the Sacred Heart," she thought. Then, pausing between the sentences, Our Lady said: "I love this devotion. By it I will to be honored."

September 10. While the Vesper bells were ringing, Our Lady showed herself and said: "If people would only pray! I give them the example." Then she joined her hands and was gone.

September 15. Our Lady spoke to Estelle in confidence, then she went on: "I have noted the attempt you are making to regain serenity. . . . There is not that serenity in the Church as a whole that I wish to see in it. . . . France will suffer."

November 1. On the occasion of this twelfth apparition, Our Lady wore the scapular of which we have spoken, but she said not a single word.

November 4. "I have chosen you," said the heavenly vision. "For the sake of my glory I have chosen the little and the weak."

November 11. On this day Estelle had made a scapular like that which Our Lady had worn at each of her last visits, and the girl was congratulated on this: "You have not been wasting your time today; you have worked for me. . . . You must make many more." Five people were with Estelle at this time.

December 8. This was the fifteenth and last apparition. It took place in the morning after Mass, and a dozen people were with Estelle. Our Lady said: "You shall see me no more. I have selected you to spread my glory and to make this devotion [i.e., that of the scapular] known. You are to go to the bishop and show him the scapular you have made. Behold the graces I will grant to those who wear it with confident faith." An abundant flood of light came forth from Our Lady's extended hands, and each drop of this flood represented a grace. The heavenly visitant then walked about Estelle's room "in the manner of one who is regretfully leaving some well-loved place in order to undertake a long journey." Then she departed and did not again appear.

At this time, the bishop of Bourges, in whose jurisdiction the parish of Pellevoisin lay, was Monseigneur de la Tour d'Auvergne. After an inquiry had been held, he was convinced of the miraculous nature of Estelle's restoration to health, and expressed his belief in her revelations. On July 28, 1877, after having obtained the blessing of Pius IX, he instituted canonically a confraternity of Our Lady of Mercy in the parish church at Pellevoisin, requiring that the members wear the scapular of which we have spoken. On September 9 of the following year, he sent his vicar general to bless the room in which the apparitions had taken place and to say Mass there. Many other prelates, including several cardinals (e.g., Cardinals Couillé, Richard, Toucher, Boyer and Dubois), showed great zeal in favor of Pellevoisin.

On June 2, 1922, the Abbé Salmon, who had been living in retirement in his old parish, was visited by the then pastor of Pellevoisin, Abbé Fonbaustier, and by Abbé Hervier, chaplain to the Dominican Sisters. They spoke to him of death, which seemed imminent, and Abbé Hervier said: "I call on you, before God, to tell us if you are of a mind to die believing in the truth of the apparitions of the Blessed Virgin to Estelle?"

M. Salmon replied clearly: "Yes, without any hesitation I say that I have never doubted their truth."

A week later he died at the age of eighty-two, with the reputation of one who had been a good priest and a man of prayer.

As to Estelle Faguette, she survived until August 23, 1929, when she had reached the age of eighty-four. She had borne all the trials and sufferings that Our Lady had promised would be hers, and the greater portion of her lifetime had been passed in prayer.

12

⁂

Fatima

(1917)

ON MAY 23, 1917, three children were watching their grazing sheep at Cova da Iria, about a mile from Fatima (Portugal). They were Francesco Marto, nine years old, his sister, Jacinta, seven, and Lucia Dos Santos, ten. Toward noon they said the rosary together and then they went back to the games they had interrupted.

All at once the sky was torn by a flash of lightning; a storm was coming. The little shepherds hastened to gather their flocks together in order that they might return to the village. While they were going down the side of the mountain, they were dazzled by a second flash of lightning. When they looked around afterward they saw a most beautiful young woman standing above a small live oak. They were frightened, and they made ready to run off, but the apparition called them back most graciously.

"Do not be afraid," she said; "come closer: I will not harm you."

The children obeyed and looked at her more closely. She seemed to be about eighteen years old. Her face was perfectly proportioned, and it surpassed the beauty of any face they had ever seen. She wore a robe and a mantle of white bordered in gold, a mantle that covered her head and fell down to her feet. Her hands were joined and held a rosary. Her whole body, and especially her face, was resplendent with "a light more beautiful and brighter than the sun." The children were dazzled by this, and were obliged at times to veil their eyes.

Lucia, who was the oldest, asked the Lady:

"Who are you and what do you want?"

"I come from heaven, and I wish to see you here on the thirteenth day of each of the next five months at this same hour. In October I will tell you who I am and what it is that I wish."

The little girl asked if she and her cousins would go to heaven.

"Yes, if you will say your rosary every day."

"Will you not give us some sign so that people may know that you have appeared to us?"

"On October 13 I will grant you a miracle."

The little shepherds faithfully kept all the appointments the Lady had made. All, that is, except the one on August 13 and this was the fault of the prefect of police of Villa Nova. He was very much annoyed at the idea of Our Lady having appeared without permission in a place that was under his jurisdiction. He was unable, of course, to do anything to her, but the children at least were in his power. On the morning of August 13, he went to the children's home under the pretext of taking them to Cova da Iria in his car. His real intention was to keep them under his own surveillance for two days and thus "outwit," as it were, the Blessed Virgin. But she was to have the last word: she simply postponed her appearance until the eighteenth and, at that time, showed herself at Valinhos (the little vales), another part of the plateau, where the shepherds were watching their flocks that day.

Before describing the miracle of October 13, we will

review the main points of the interrogation to which Lucia was subjected on September 27 by the Vicomte de Montelo, a priest of the diocese of Santarem.

"Is it really true that Our Lady appeared to you at Cova da Iria?"

"Yes, it is."

"How many times?"

"Five; once each month."

"On which day of the month?"

"Always on the 13th, except in August when I was arrested and taken to Villa Nova by the prefect of police. That month I did not see her until some days later at Valinhos."

"From what direction does she come? Does she come from the east?"

"I know nothing of that; I have not seen her come from either side. She appears over the live oak, and when she goes away she goes in the direction of the rising sun."

"How long does she stay?"

"This varies; sometimes not longer than it takes to say a *Pater,* much less to be able to get through the rosary."

"Were you not afraid when you first saw her?"

"Oh yes, I even wished to run off with Jacinta and Francesco, but she said that we had nothing to fear, that she would not hurt us."

"How is she dressed?"

"She wears a white robe which goes from her head down to her feet. She is covered with a cloak of the same color and as long as her robe."

"Is her robe decorated in any way?"

"We could see two golden strands which fell from her neck to her waist and were joined there by a golden tassel."

"Does she wear earrings?"

"Yes, little ones."

"In which hand does she hold her rosary?"

"In her right hand."

"Does it have a cross?"

"Yes, the cross and the beads of the rosary are all of white."

"Have you ever asked her what her name is?"

"Yes, and she said to me: 'I shall not tell you my name before October 13.' "

"Did you ask whence she came?"

"I said to her: 'Where do you come from?' and she replied: 'From heaven.' "

"Was she happy or sad?"

"Sometimes I have seen her smiling and sometimes looking sad, but she is always serious."

"Did she advise you or your cousins to recite any prayers?"

"Yes, she urged us to say the beads in honor of Our Lady of the Rosary for the peace of the world."

"Is it true that she has told you a secret and has forbidden you to reveal it?"

"That is true."

"Is it something that concerns you alone?"

"It concerns all three of us."

"Can you not reveal it even to your confessor?"

To this question the little girl made no answer, and the priest, seeing her embarrassment, decided it would be as well not to insist.

"It has been said that in order to put an end to the tiresome questions of the prefect on the day of your arrest, you told him, as the secret, something that was not true, and that you have boasted of having deceived him. Is this true?"

"It is not so. The prefect wanted to know the secret; but since I had been forbidden to reveal it, I would not tell him. I told him all the rest of what Our Lady had said to me. Perhaps he may have thought that I had told him everything, but I did not do so. And I never wished to deceive him."

"Is it true that Our Lady suggested that you should learn how to read?"

"Yes, the second time she appeared she told me this."

"Did she also tell you that she would take you to heaven in October? Why then would you need to know how to read?"

"None of this is true. Our Lady never said that she would take me to heaven next October."

"What did Our Lady have to say about the money that was placed at the foot of the live oak in the Cova da Iria?"

"She said that it was to be put into two barrows; that I was to take one to the parish church with the help of Jacinta and two other little girls, and that Francesco was to take the other to the same place with the help of three of his young friends. This money was to be set aside either for celebrating the feast of Our Lady of the Rosary or for building a chapel."

"Are you glad that Our Lady has appeared to you?"

"I am very glad."

"On the 13th of October will Our Lady come alone?"

"No, St. Joseph also will come, and the Child Jesus as well; and a little later, peace will be given to the world."

"Has Our Lady revealed anything else to you?"

"She said that on October 13 she will work a miracle, a great miracle, so that the whole world may know that she has actually appeared."

"Why is it that during the apparitions you so frequently lower your eyes and look away from the Lady?"

"Because sometimes her brightness blinds me."

"Has she taught you any prayer?"

"Yes, she has taught me a prayer that she wishes us to recite after each decade of the rosary."

"Do you know this prayer by heart?"

"*My Jesus, forgive us our sins, save us from the fires of hell, and comfort the souls in purgatory, especially those who are most abandoned.*"

On October 13, at noon, seventy thousand people were there to observe the miracle which had been announced. It rained. Lucia asked that all umbrellas be shut. This was done. The rain stopped. The Virgin then showed herself to the children. Then all at once the clouds rolled away, the sun came out, and the crowd was greatly astonished to see it wheel around with dizzying speed while shooting out flames in the manner of a fine display of fireworks. It could be described as a wheel of fire, and successively it took on all the colors of the rainbow. This phenomenon which no one had previously seen, and which had not been recorded by the instruments in observatories, was repeated three times and lasted for ten minutes. At one moment, it seemed that the sun fell from the sky and was cast to the earth. Seeing this, the crowd fell to their knees. They cried out and wept, beat their breasts, asked forgiveness and said the *Credo* and the *Ave Maria*. Then the sun reverted to its normal brightness.

That same day, at seven in the evening, Canon Formigao questioned the children again. Their replies were consistent, but what Lucia had to say was by far of the greatest significance. Here is the substance of her answers.

"Is it true that the Virgin has appeared to you today at Cova da Iria?"

"Yes."

"Was she dressed in the same way as before?"

"She wore the same robes."

"Is it true that you also saw St. Joseph and the Child Jesus?"

"Yes, this is true."

"Have you seen any other apparitions?"

"Our Lord appeared also to bless the people, and Our Lady appeared in two ways."

"What do you mean by 'in two ways?' "

"I mean that she appeared dressed like the Mother of Sorrows but without the sword in her heart. Later she was like the Virgin of Carmel."

"Did you see all these apparitions at the same time?"

"No, first I saw Our Lady of the Rosary, St. Joseph and the Child Jesus, then Our Lord alone; afterward the Mother of Sorrows; finally someone who seemed to me to be the Virgin of Carmel."

"Was the Child Jesus standing or was He on the arm of St. Joseph?"

"On the arm of St. Joseph."

"Was the child big?"

"No, he was very small."

"What age could he have been?"

"About a year old."

"Did they also appear above the live oak?"

"No, they appeared near the sun after the Virgin had gone away from the bush."

"Was Our Lord standing?"

"I saw only the upper part of His body."

"How long did the apparition above the bush last? Was there enough time to say the rosary?"

"It seemed to me that there was not time enough."

"Did the personages you saw near the sun remain a long while?"

"No, they stayed only for a short time."

"Did the Lady tell you who she was?"

"She told me that she was Our Lady of the Rosary."

"Did you ask her what she wanted?"

"Yes, I did ask her. She said that we were to be converted, that we should not further offend Our Lord who has already been too often offended, that we ought to say the rosary and ask forgiveness of our sins."

"Was there nothing else?"

"She also asked that a chapel be built at Cova da Iria."

"Did she have anything to say about our soldiers who have died in the war?"

"No, she did not speak of them."

"Did she express a wish that people do penance?"

"Yes."

"Did she actually use the word 'penance?' "

"No, she did not use this word; she said that we should say the rosary, amend our lives, and ask Our Lord to forgive us our sins."

"Was it before or after the disappearance of the Lady that the miracle of the sun began?"

"It was after."

"Did you see the Lady appear?"

"Yes."

"And did you also see her go?"

"Yes."

"In leaving, did she withdraw facing the crowd or did she turn her back on them?"

"She turned her back on them."

"Do you believe that she will appear again?"

"I do not count on seeing her again; but it is a subject on which she has said nothing."

"Will the Virgin not work other miracles? Will she not cure the sick?"

"I do not know."

"Have you not asked some favors of her?"

"I told her today that I had several requests to make. She replied that she would grant some, but not the others."

"When she appeared near the sun, of what color were her robes?"

"Her veil was blue and her robe white."

"What colors were worn by Our Lord, by St. Joseph and by the Child Jesus?"

"They wore red robes."

The results of the events of October 13 were decisive, and pilgrims began to come in great numbers. The chapel for which Our Lady had asked was begun in 1919; but it was not until 1921 that the ecclesiastical authorities gave permission for services to be held on the mountain. Some months later a spring gushed up, and it has not yet ceased to flow. Henceforth, the ground was marked by the trampling feet of many pilgrims. Once more, the civil powers and the anticlerical press gave evidence of their ill-will in regard to the spring, the pilgrimages and the prayers. On May 13, 1920, the police and the Army were even ordered to bar the roads leading to Cova da Iria. The journalists fulminated in characteristic fashion while, faithful to their usual habits, the anarchists tried to blow up the chapel in

March 1922. All these efforts were in vain: on the thirteenth of the following May sixty thousand persons prayed in the open air. Since then the pilgrims are numbered by hundreds of thousands. Together with Lourdes, Fatima has become the most frequented popular place of pilgrimage in the Christian world.

As for the children who saw the apparitions, they continued at first to guard their flocks, and were faithful in saying the rosary as well. Then death separated them. In December 1918 Francesco caught the grippe. It was thought that he would recover, but he himself declared with certainty that he would never be well, and on April 5, 1919, he died, in his tenth year. Some months afterward, his sister Jacinta fell a victim to pleurisy. She was taken to Lisbon for an operation. She expressed the opinion that the operation would **not** help, inasmuch as Our Lady had foretold her early death. And so it turned out, for the child died on February 20, 1920, at the age of ten.

Lucia is the only one of three who is still alive (1958). In 1921 she began to study under the Sisters of St. Dorothy, and in 1928 she entered their congregation. She remained with them until 1948, but in that year withdrew from their ranks in order to become a Carmelite nun in the convent of Coimbra, where she is known as Sister Mary of the Immaculate Heart. It is said that she has been favored with further revelations and visions.

13

Beauraing

(1932–1933)

BEAURAING (Namur, Belgium) is situated a few miles from the French frontier, and had about 2,400 inhabitants in 1932. The way leading from the village and going toward Rochefort and the Grottoes of Han passes under the railway line. On the right, before one comes to the viaduct, there can be seen in the background the house of the Sisters of Christian Doctrine of Nancy, whose grounds abut a high slope. A little flower garden, with some trees and a small replica of the Lourdes grotto, extends down to the road from which it is separated by a grille.

Such is the setting in which the Virgin showed herself thirty-five times between November 29, 1932, and January 3, 1933. At first she appeared walking on the viaduct, but on the following days she was seen near the grille in a rose hawthorn bush, about thirty feet away from the grotto.

Of the five children who saw her here, two belonged to the Degeimbre family: Andrée (fourteen) and Gilberte (thirteen). Three were members of the Voisin family: Fernande (fifteen), Gilberte (thirteen) and Albert (eleven). Their two families were respectable but scarcely devout, and even the children themselves were not outstanding for their piety, although they were well behaved, and their trustworthiness had never been questioned.

I myself stood beside them during one of the apparitions. Afterward, we returned to the place and were able to question the children at length, as well as their parents, priests, teachers and many others who knew them. It was after the inquiry that the following report was drawn up. It is in agreement with other inquiries that have been made.

The Apparitions

Tuesday, November 29, 1932. Gilberte Voisin was a day student with the Sisters of Christian Doctrine, and being only thirteen, was not allowed to go home from the convent alone. Ordinarily, it was her father who went to fetch her, but on this day it was her brother and sister, together with their friends the Degeimbre children who came through the garden gate and started toward the convent at about six-thirty. Albert rang the bell and then turned around while waiting for the door to be opened. Suddenly he cried out: "Look at the statue in the garden: it is walking about above the bridge!" Without looking the little girls said, "What you see must be the headlights of an auto." Then they, too, saw that the statue had seemingly left the grotto and was walking along the railroad track. Meanwhile, the Sister Superior came to open the door, bringing Gilberte with her. She laughed at what the children told her and closed the door again. When they returned to the grille they saw the apparition again and ran off, not daring to lift their eyes. Gilberte now saw the strange walker and fell as she ran. Her companions turned back to pick her up and saw that the Lady still remained on the slope. Hurriedly, they all went home.

Wednesday, November 30. At about six-thirty Our Lady showed herself at four different places. When the children reached the grille, they saw her there; when they rang, they saw her above a holly bush; when they were leaving the convent, they saw her on the viaduct; and as they were returning home they saw her near the house of the Saim-pain family.

Their parents wished to put an end to these visions. They consulted among themselves, and it was decided that all would go back to the place with the exception of the two Gilbertes. Scarcely had the little band reached the grille when the three children saw the Lady of the former apparitions. This time she was standing perfectly still. They wept; they cried out; they were told rather to pray; they fell upon their knees and recited an *Ave*. Then the mother of the Degeimbre children decided to walk closer to the grotto to assure herself whether or not the statue had moved. "Wait, Mother," Andrée suddenly called out, "do not go closer; you will offend her!" The children added that they had not spoken of the statue in the grotto, be-cause this time the Lady they saw did not resemble it in any way.

Friday, December 2. On this day Gilberte Voisin's father went himself to fetch his daughter and then took her to the Degeimbre home. From there, in company with a dozen people, the children walked back to the convent. Someone suggested to Albert that he should ask the appari-tion her name. When the little group came to the grille, the five children saw the Lady and at once all fell to their knees and recited the *Ave Maria*.

"Are you the Immaculate Virgin?" asked Albert.

The Lady, who was very beautiful with blue eyes and a serious face lightened by a smile, seemed to be between eighteen and twenty years of age. She wore a long, white, pleated robe, that gave off a reflection of sky blue. A rosary hung from her arm. She was in an attitude of prayer, eyes raised and hands joined. When she spoke to the children she looked down in their direction, and when she finished speaking she opened her arms as if to embrace them.

In answer to Albert's question, she inclined her head to signify assent.

"What do you want of us?" asked the little boy.

"That you be really good," she replied.

Françoise cried: "We will be."

When the apparition reoccurred at about half-past eight, it was again Albert who spoke to her:

"Are you really the Immaculate Virgin?"

Again she made an affirmative sign with her head.

"What do you want of us?" said he.

"Is it true that you will always be good?"

"Yes, we always will be," said the little boy.

Then, opening her arms, the apparition disappeared and the children fell back into the crowd. One of the young men who was in the company began to search the bushes with an electric torch. Albert came behind him and knelt down again, crying out: "There she is!" He recited an *Ave* and said that Our Lady had smiled at him. For the children themselves, it was not a matter to doubt: in their eyes it was indeed Our Lady who had appeared on the large bough of the hawthorn. This conviction remained unshaken: every evening they returned to the scene hoping once again to see her, hoping that she would cure the uncle of the Degeimbres who was blind and also that she would cure their paralyzed fellow student, Joseph Degondenne.

Saturday, December 3. The Sisters felt far from pleased at the spectacle for which their garden had become the theater. To put an end to the matter, the Superior ap-

pointed someone to take Gilberte home, thus depriving
the other children of the excuse they had for coming into
the garden and falling into ecstasies before the bush. If
they were obstinate they would find someone to talk to:
the two watchdogs who guarded the convent were un-
leashed and the police alerted. These threats were enough
to cause the children to stay at home; however, Albert
declared that he felt very unhappy going to bed that night,
and Andrée so far forgot herself as to wish that the Sisters'
dogs might be dead on the morrow.

Sunday, December 4. Although the Sister Superior had
herself determined to take Gilberte home, the children
were at the grille at about seven o'clock, and with them
were the blind uncle and the little crippled boy. Our
Lady appeared to them. They knelt and prayed.

Speaking in unison, they said: "If you wish to grant us
a favor, we beg you to cure Joseph Degondenne and our
blind uncle."

And Albert, in his anxiety to help with the miracle,
added the question: "On what day shall we come?"

"On the feast of the Immaculate Conception," replied
the Virgin.

"Ought we build a chapel in your honor?" asked Fernande to whom it appeared that the apparition was about
to make a request.

"Yes," smiled the Virgin, inclining her head.

Monday, December 5. The happenings at Beauraing
had begun to arouse interest throughout the countryside
and a great crowd had gathered on the road opposite the
convent when the children arrived at about 6:30 on this
day. Again it was Albert who acted as spokesman:

"If you are the Immaculate Virgin, we beg you to
work all the miracles you can next Thursday, in the full
sight of all."

He received no reply, so he asked again. But the Virgin remained silent, and as the children began to cry Albert grew more insistent:

"When, then, do you wish us to return?"

"In the evening," she replied.

"We will be here," promised the little boy.

And at about 8:30 that same day they did return. Twice they saw the apparition, and on each occasion the scene followed an unvarying pattern.

The Scene

On that cold December night the five children came wearing heavy boots and wrapped up in shawls and great-coats. The older ones were on foot, and the two younger children followed the crowd borne in the arms of some strong villagers. They stood before the grille outside the garden, and looked at the hawthorn bush without paying any attention to the physicians or to the people who thronged around. At once they began the rosary in that psalmodic tone that one usually hears in the churches of France. Then, suddenly, they fell on their knees at the same time; their hands remained at chin level as though restrained in a vise; their voices rang out in a higher register but pantingly. Their gaze was fixed and their faces became beautiful and, as it were, transfigured, as they sang out the words of the *Ave Maria* in rapid rhythm, one word following closely upon another. The Virgin was there! They saw her, they felt her presence, and they rejoiced in it; they were rapt out of themselves. It was no longer the rosary passing through their set fingers which they recited: the *Paters* and *Glorias* were forgotten; their clear voices rang out in an overlapping chain of *Aves* almost as if they were some magical formula by which they hoped to retain the supernatural Presence. A silence charged with emotion gripped the crowd. The incantatory note did not long endure. Soon in the course of an *Ave*, the twelfth, the seventeenth, the thirtieth, the voices suddenly fell in a sound of disappointment. The smiling Virgin had vanished: the children were again conscious of being in the world; they stood up, they were themselves again, and they resumed in the customary rhythm the psalmody of the interrupted rosary.

The Virgin having left, the children were seized upon by the physicians. Throughout the scene of the apparition these men had been closely watching the children, and now that it was over, they separated them from one another in order to be certain that they were not in collusion and each child in turn was questioned alone. The jury before whom they appeared was greater on some days, lesser on others. At times there were no more than six physicians, at others as many as forty, sixty or even more. Each one put his own questions to the children, and tried to make them contradict each other, while a notary took down the queries and the answers made to them. These latter were ordinarily identical. When they differed it was not because one child disagreed with another, but because each reported something intended for himself alone.

Tuesday, December 6. As soon as the apparition had begun, the blind uncle cried out: "I can neither see nor hear you; tell the children what I must do to be cured."

"Tell us on what day we are to come!" said Albert.

"*On the feast of the Immaculate Conception,*" replied Our Lady who remained that evening throughout the reci-

tation of the rosary, and then returned for a second time
two hours later.

Wednesday, December 7. Someone having placed himself between Fernande and the hawthorn bush, the little
girl bent forward so that she might not lose sight of the
apparition.

Thursday, December 8. Great hopes had been raised for
the feast of the Immaculate Conception, and an immense
crowd was present. The Virgin herself was there at six
o'clock. "Grant that I may see!" cried the blind man.
"Grant that I may walk!" begged the little victim of
paralysis. The children called out: "Speak to us, please,
for you have promised.'" When they received no reply,
they wept. The physicians subjected them to various tests:
they scratched their temples with a knife, they pinched
their cheeks sharply; they held lighted matches to their
hands, and finally they flashed their electric torches into
their eyes. But far from provoking any notice on the part
of the children, the physicians might as well have done
none of these things, nor were any traces later found of
marks of pinches, scratches or burns. Otherwise, nothing
more took place, nor did the Virgin return when the children came again before the bush at about nine o'clock.
Nor was anything seen of the apparition on the four following days.

Tuesday, December 13. The usual scene took place
and one of the physicians again scratched Gilberte Voisin
with his pocket knife, but she said to him: "Let me be;
it is on your account that the Blessed Virgin has gone
away!" Then she spoke to the vision: "Sweet Virgin, come
back when we are alone."

Wednesday, December 14. This was like the preceding

day except for the incident noted above. Then there followed two days on which nothing happened, the fifteenth and sixteenth.

Saturday, December 17. A Jesuit who visited Beauraing suggested to the children that they question the Virgin "in the name of the clergy" about her wishes. They accepted this counsel, and called out:

"In the name of the clergy, we beg you to say what they ought to do for you."

"A chapel," said the apparition.

"Yes, we will have it built."

On the next day, Sunday, there was no vision.

Monday, December 19, and Tuesday, December 20. On the preceding Saturday it had been Andrée who had seemed to be first aware of the Lady's coming. Today, Monday, it was Fernande who first raised her voice. The hasty cantering of the *Aves* went on until the twenty-ninth *"Je vous salue, Marie,"* of which, indeed, only the first word was heard, so that even the mute "e" did not seem to follow the characteristic sound of the "j" as plainly pronounced. The next day, Tuesday, Our Lady arrived after they had waited for seventeen minutes and she remained during the recitation of twenty-nine *Aves.*

Wednesday, December 21. "Tell us who you are," asked the children.

"I am the Immaculate Virgin," responded the apparition in a way that was audible to three of them; Gilberte Degeimbre saw her lips move but heard nothing while Albert Voisin had only a confused recollection of it all.

Thursday, December 22. Care was taken to cast light on the hawthorn bush as though in full daylight. Nevertheless, four of the children saw the Virgin appear among its branches. The eighteen physicians who were present noted that Albert went down on his knees after the little girls. He afterward stated that in spite of this he had "seen nothing today."

Friday, December 23. Albert again saw nothing. At the suggestion of Dr. Maistriaux, Fernande asked this question:

"Why have you come?"

"So that pilgrims may come here."

The other three little girls did not hear this reply.

Saturday, December 24. Once again the apparition was questioned. Gilberte Voisin asked:

"Since you are the Immaculate Virgin, will you soon give us a sign?"

And immediately Andrée Degeimbre added the plea: "If you are the Immaculate Virgin, will you not prove it to us?"

But Our Lady did not reply to these questions. Albert alone asserted that he had heard her say "Yes."

Sunday, December 25. This being Christmas, the children hoped particularly to have a visit from their heavenly friend, but she came neither on this day nor on the day after.

On *Tuesday, December 27,* they saw her at a later hour than was usual, that is to say at about nine forty-five.

Wednesday, December 28. Evidently, the children at once realized that the Madonna had something to say, for they cried out together:

"Speak, we are listening."

"*Very soon, the last apparition will take place,*" said the Virgin.

On the following day there was something new: Fernande saw a heart of gold surrounded by great rays of light revealed on Our Lady's breast as she reached out her arms at the moment of leaving them.

The next day, the four little girls all saw the heart.

For a moment Fernande was silent, and she later explained it was because she heard the apparition say: *"Pray, pray much!"*

Sunday, December 31. Finally, Albert too saw that the Virgin had a golden heart. Fifteen thousand people had gathered along the road at the time of the first apparition on this day. I say the first, because two others followed, one at about nine forty-five, and the other at about ten o'clock.

Sunday, January 1, 1933. Albert was slow in kneeling, as I myself observed; he prayed in a haphazard way and turned around to tell me that he had "his knee on a very sharp stone." When questioned, it appeared that he had neither seen nor heard anything. His sister, Gilberte, had seen the Virgin, and moreover she had heard her say: *"Pray always."* Fernande saw only the movement of her lips but heard nothing. Andrée thought that the apparition had wanted to say something. Gilberte Degeimbre had seen the Virgin and no more. Those who were near the children were struck by the amount of force, even of violence, which was required to detach them from the ground after the vision: the two Gilbertes seemed rooted to the earth.

Monday, January 2. The apparition was seen at about seven-thirty. After three of the children stopped praying, Gilberte Voisin said three more *Aves:* the vision had been prolonged in her case. It was also noted that Fernande had stopped for a moment as if to listen. She said that the Virgin had confided to her: *"Tomorrow, I will say something to each one of you in particular."*

Tuesday, January 3. The morning papers broadcast the news that on that evening each of the children was to receive a special message. What would it be? was the question that twenty-four physicians and twenty-five thousand curious onlookers asked themselves. The scene unfolded in its customary fashion, except that Fernande knelt down after the others, and when she prayed her voice did not rise to a high pitch. It was noted also that the other four stopped for a moment and then resumed their recitation of the *Ave Maria*. What did this mean? It was soon to become known.

Now that the vision had disappeared, Fernande wore an air of disappointment, and seemed sad. Dr. Maistriaux noticed this, and in a fatherly way he prescribed another rosary. However, this did not provide the needed remedy. The disappointed little girl remained in front of the hawthorn bush while the four others went to sing a hymn before the grotto. All at once, she fell to her knees, fastened, as it were, to the earth, and she began to cry out the *Ave Maria* in a loud voice. Then she stopped, as if listening, with her body bent forward. Finally, she seemed transported and said "Yes, yes," to the apparition, and immediately she broke into sobs. The singing of the hymn had ceased: a chill passed over the crowd. What had happened? The result of the interrogation was to show Our Lady had taken leave of the children as she had foretold. To Andrée she had said: *"I am the Mother of God, the Queen of Heaven, pray always, farewell."* To Gilberte Voisin: *"I will convert sinners. Farewell."* To Gilberte Degeimbre and Albert Voisin: *"Farewell."* It was learned, moreover, that secret messages had been confided to three of them, the two Gilbertes and Albert. The little boy had received two, one of which he was never to reveal, and the other so sad that he did not know if he could bear to speak of it. As to Fernande, she had seen nothing whatever at first, but at the end the Virgin had appeared to her alone.

"Do you love my Son?" she had asked.

"Yes," replied the little girl in rapture.

"Do you love me?"

"Yes."

"Then for my sake, practice self-denial."

With these final words the apparition vanished.

And after this, despite the fact that the children returned thousands of times to the hawthorn bush, she was not again seen by any of them.

Decree of the Ordinary

For a quite a time, a certain religious, backed by a medical man, an alienist, showed extraordinary zeal in contesting the truth of the apparitions of Beauraing. But neither his ardor nor his arguments were able to shake the belief of sensible people who were, moreover, better informed than he, and he finally abandoned his campaign.

The inquiry undertaken by ecclesiasiastical authority went on for ten years, after which Monseigneur Charue, bishop of Namur, published a decree authorizing the faithful publicly to venerate Our Lady of Beauraing. On July 18, 1947, Pope Pius XII stated that he blessed from his heart the shrine that had been erected and the pilgrimages that were being made. Since then each year has seen between five and six hundred thousand people betake themselves to Beauraing to pray to the Virgin of the golden heart. Many conversions have taken place through this devotion, and among the cures obtained, two were the object of a very careful canonical inquiry and were declared "miraculous" by Monseigneur Charue. On July 2, 1949, the same prelate issued a new decree declaring that "it is entirely safe to affirm that the Queen of Heaven has appeared to the children of Beauraing."

All of the children are married and have children of their own. They have agreed never to make public profit of what they have seen. Some of them have already known much suffering; all continue to lead Christian lives.

14

Banneux

(1933)

SCARCELY had the apparitions at Beauraing come to an end when others occurred at Banneux, about thirty miles southeast of Liége (Belgium) and not far from the German frontier.

In this small Belgian village of about three hundred inhabitants, the practice of religion had fallen into neglect at the time of which we speak. This was particularly true of the Beco family whose humble cottage stood off by itself, facing a pine wood, at a distance of about a half mile from the other houses in the village. In this cottage there lived an honest workman who, despite zealous labor, was scarcely able to support his wife and their seven children.

Mariette, the eldest of his family, was approaching her twelfth year; she was neither more nor less endowed than the majority of girls of her age, but was more taciturn and more withdrawn. She had rarely been to school, not even to catechism classes; she no longer went to Mass and it seems that she had never even made her first Communion. However, in the opinion of the best judges, she was a perfectly sane and normal girl whose open face showed her goodness of soul and rectitude of conscience. "Nevertheless," writes Monseigneur Kerhofs, bishop of Liége, "in the whole village she was the child who seemed to be the farthest from God, and the least prepared for any kind of mystical manifestation."

Yet it was she whom the Virgin chose as confidant and favored with eight apparitions at the beginning of the year 1933.

Sunday, January 15. The first of these apparitions took place on Sunday, January 15, and like those which followed, occurred at about seven in the evening.

While her father was resting in bed in the next room and her mother was engaged in household cares in the kitchen, Mariette was sitting on a bench near the window of the same room. From time to time, she would rise, kneel upon the bench, and lift up the bedspread that served as a curtain for the window to watch for the return of her ten-year-old brother Julien. He had been gone since midday and because he had not yet returned she was anxious about him. An icy wind was roaring without, bending the tops of the pines which were heavy with snow. Suddenly on this night unlit by the moon, a young and most beautiful Lady appeared, shining with radiance, in the little garden that separated the house from the road. Her hands joined and wearing a blue girdle, she stood motionless on a hummock of earth.

"I thought that it was an illusion produced by the reflection of the gas lamp that stood on the table," said Mariette, "so I took the lamp into the other room, shut the door and went back to the window to look again. The lovely Lady was still there. I called my mother, but she made fun of me. I said two or three decades of my rosary with my eyes fixed on the apparition which smiled at me and made me a sign to come nearer. My mother locked the door to prevent me from going out. I looked through the window once more, but the Lady had gone. It seems to me that she had remained in the garden for about ten minutes. At first I was afraid, but then I felt reassured."

On the following Wednesday Mariette heard Mass and went to the catechism class that she had given up attending. Moreover, she, who had never known her lesson, knew it now. When the catechism lesson was over, the chaplain of Banneux, Abbé Jamin, having been warned by one of Mariette's friends, put her through a long interrogation in which he did all he could to weaken her faith in the vision and to insure her silence on the subject.

Wednesday, January 18. Mariette felt herself impelled to go to pray in the place where the apparition had taken place. It was eleven degrees below zero, but the girl, who was in ecstasy, held out her arms to the Virgin and paid no attention to cold or darkness, or to the repeated calls of her father. He saw the child arise and begin to walk.

"Where are you going?" he asked. "Come in!"

"She is calling me," replied Mariette, going on in the manner of a sleep walker. The Virgin led her toward a little spring that flowed about a hundred yards away, at the edge of the wood.

"Put your hands in the water," the Virgin said to her.

Mariette did so, and like one in a dream she repeated the words she had heard.

"This spring is set aside for me," remarked the Virgin. Then she said "Good night" and *Au revoir* to the child and disappeared. On this day, the apparition had lasted for about half an hour.

On the following morning, just as if he were doing nothing unusual, Beco the workman went to confession and Communion.

Thursday, January 19. At the same hour and in the same part of the garden, Mariette knelt down, prayed, and almost immediately opened her arms and cried out, "She is here!" It was the Virgin who, as was to be the case from henceforth, did not appear suddenly and in her usual size, but came down from heaven borne upon a cloud which appeared in the southwest. At first she seemed very small; but she grew in size as she neared the earth, so that by the time she came before the child she had regained her normal stature.

As she had been advised, Mariette asked:

"Who are you, lovely Lady?"

"I am the Virgin of the Poor," replied the apparition.

Once again the child was led toward the spring, and there she asked: "Yesterday you said: 'This spring is set aside for me' . . . Why did you say 'for me?' "

"This spring is set aside for all peoples in order that the sick may be helped," replied the Virgin.

"Thank you! Thank you!" said Mariette who, as she always did, repeated loudly and as soon as she heard them the words spoken by the beautiful Lady.

"I will pray for you," the Lady said. *"Au revoir!"*

On this occasion the apparition lasted only about seven minutes. The Virgin had not ceased to smile, but as she began to leave she became smaller and smaller and went away between the treetops in the same direction she had come.

There were several witnesses to this scene; but those present never numbered more than twenty. When they returned to the house one of the witnesses explained to Mariette by means of a map of the world who were *les nations* (i.e., "all peoples"), a term she had not been able to understand.

Friday, January 20. "What do you wish, my lovely Lady?"

"I would like a little chapel."

Having said this, the Virgin laid her hands on the little girl and blessed her, and then she disappeared.

Saturday, February 11. Although the weather had been extremely cold, Mariette had gone every evening into the garden to recite the rosary; but the Virgin did not again appear until this day. Once more she led the child to the spring where she said again: "I am come to relieve suffer-ing."

Wednesday, February 15. "Blessed Virgin," said Mari-ette to Our Lady, who appeared as she was reciting the rosary, "our chaplain has requested me to ask you for a sign."

"Trust me. . . . I will trust you. . . . Pray much," was the Virgin's response. "*Au revoir.*"

Then she confided a secret which Mariette was not to reveal to anyone — a secret which, in fact, she has care-fully kept — and the Lady again took leave of her young friend, saying "*Au revoir.*"

Monday, February 20. For the fourth and final time the apparition took Mariette to the spring. There she made anew this recommendation: "My dear child, pray much," and before leaving her said "*Au revoir.*"

Thursday, March 2. The rain had been falling for a long time but it suddenly ceased as Mariette came to the third decade of her rosary. She saw the apparition return, al-though this time the Virgin was not smiling. She even seemed somewhat sad.

"I am the Mother of the Saviour, the Mother of God," said the Virgin. "Pray much."

She then confided certain things to her which Mariette has never revealed. Then she said: "Farewell," laying her hands on the girl in blessing, and withdrew. The child, who understood that this was the final farewell, got up from her knees, stood up to her full height and raised her arms, then she fell prostrate on the ground. Her father lifted her up and carried her into the house. She wept for a very long time, keeping her eyes covered with her hands, as she lay on the bed where he had placed her. When her tears had ceased, the women gathered around her asked her what had caused her to cry so much. She said: "The Blessed Virgin will not return again. She has told me 'Farewell.' "

The duty of judging these happenings was remitted by the Holy Office to the bishop of Liége, and in 1942 he approved the veneration of Our Lady of Banneux. But it was not until after the conclusion of a lengthy investigation that, in a pastoral letter of August 22, 1949, he declared that "the reality of the eight apparitions can and should be unreservedly acknowledged."

He gave Our Lady what she had asked for, and she herself has not failed to grant what she has promised. A "little chapel" was built in the place she had pointed out. Built of local rubble, and, like the workmen's houses that stand nearby, covered with blue slate, it now contains more than two thousand *ex voto* offerings. The spring "set aside for her" still flows at the edge of the wood, and its waters have been carried afar that they may "relieve the sick of all nations." A number of institutions have been established for the sick and the needy who are drawn to this place. Here religious of various congregations devote themselves to the care of the sick poor, priests work zealously among them, and the many lay people who come derive great benefits from retreats.

Each year, at least two hundred and fifty thousand pilgrims come to Banneux. Not to speak of a great many conversions due to the Virgin of the Poor, we could enumerate a hundred extraordinary — if not, indeed, miraculous — cures ascribed to her intercession.

What is even more astonishing is the number of churches, shrines and monuments which, during the years, have been dedicated to her throughout the world. A list, drawn up in 1953, runs to 444. They are found in the following lands: Germany, England, Australia, Austria, Brazil, Canada, Colombia, the Congo, Ceylon, the Belgian Congo, Korea, the Ivory Coast, France, Holland, Reunion Island, Italy, the West Indies, Indonesia, the Portuguese Indies (Goa, Damão, and Diu), Ireland, Lebanon, Morocco, Mozambique, Palestine, Romania, Sweden and the Transvaal.

Like the children of Beauraing, Mariette Beco, who is now married, leads a good Christian life.

Part Three

THE SIGNIFICANCE OF
THE APPARITIONS

15

❦

The Significance of the Apparitions

Signs and Wonders

ALL that we have passed in review bears the mark of the miraculous. We have seen the Virgin come from heaven to earth in the twinkling of an eye, we have seen her pass through walls, walk above the treetops, appear in the air as though she came and went like light and shadow. She had but to show herself to turn back the German army on its march and to prolong by half a century the life of a dying woman for whom burial preparations were being made. She has cured all types of illness by means of plain water, converted sinners by means of a medal; for more than a century she has granted to the voice of a child in wooden shoes the power to call millions of people to prayer before a rock.

Such phenomena depend upon divine power. They are not astonishing to those who believe in the Scriptures. For do not the Scriptures contain the narrative of hundreds of miracles, and did not Jesus declare that He would always work such wonders? Celestial apparitions notably abound in both Old and New Testaments, and they have continued since the founding of the Church. And how many were the times when the Virgin made herself visible here and there before she appeared to Catherine Labouré! So true is this that there are not many parts of Christendom that cannot take pride in a visit from her, and where, even now, pilgrimages do not keep the memory of those visits fresh.

But the apparitions in the Rue du Bac and those that followed have, nevertheless, a special importance for us by reason of the fact that they are so recent, and because they have been well investigated and have reoccurred with such mysterious frequency; by reason, too, of the fact that they are linked together, that they complement each other, that they seem to form part of one providential design, and that their effects are prolonged before our eyes.

Therefore, it is natural that we seek to understand the reason and the significance of these divine interventions which, so to speak, are addressed to each and every one of us.

Signs and wonders. If, as Scripture asserts, miracles are signs given by God to show the authenticity of Christ's mission, it is evident that these apparitions we are considering took place only to confirm the Gospel message. Now what is the Gospel other than the revelation of our supernatural destiny and the means we are to take in order to fulfill it. One realizes from the very words of Our Lady herself that it was with the object of recalling our minds to heaven and of helping us to go there that she has come among us again.

Yet it may still be asked why between 1830 and our own time she should have done this so much more often than before. This is a question which quite properly arises, and it is one which we will first of all seek to solve.

Naturalism and the supernatural

We are frequently told by the daily press that *our civilization is the greatest of all known to history.*[1] This

1 "In our present civilization, the greatest in known history, we have

would be true enough were civilization properly measured by washing machines, electrical appliances, means of transportation and all the material comforts we possess. But in reality this is a false claim, for the greatness of a civilization is to be gauged in proportion to its spiritual, esthetic and moral values. Now who is there who would claim to see in the average of our contemporaries greater intelligence, greater gifts of the interior life and greater refine‑ment than could be found in an earlier time? Or who can say that modern civilization has borne more beautiful fruit or produced greater men than those that have gone before? As far as religious genius is concerned, have we surpassed Francis of Assisi or St. Augustine? As to philosophers, psychologists, moralists, whom can we place beside Plato, Epictetus, Pascal and the author of the *Imitation*? Among writers, which of the modernists is the equal of Isaiah, Homer, Dante or Shakespeare? Among artists, who of our day is likely to eclipse Bach and Mozart, Rembrandt and Raphael, Phidias, Michelangelo and the builders of the cathedrals? So far as sociological and charitable works are concerned, it cannot be said that we have particularly excelled, for not even the most barbaric times exceeded the hate and the massacres of our day.

Of course, we must admit that if our age is inferior to others in the realm of the spirit, its superiority in the domain of the material cannot be denied. Now, the very first of the apparitions we have described dates from the beginnings of our modern scientific and industrial era. It was around those years that scientists were beginning to discover all sorts of natural laws that were unknown be‑fore, laws that technicians, on their part, made haste to

---

ideas of mechanical, electrical and atomic power." — Charles R. Titus, professor of political sciences at UCLA, Los Angeles *Times*, September 29, 1957.

put into use. They applied their new knowledge on earth, on sea, in the air, in factories, in cookery, in pharmacy, in surgeries, in theaters and elsewhere. It is to them that we owe railroads, automobiles, airplanes, anesthetics, nylon, plastic, radar, television, refrigeration, electric razors, explosives, the machine gun and countless other wonderful inventions useful in both peace and war, not to mention the atomic interplanetary machines now being brought to perfection. All this would be well enough were man not unhappily in the grip of two defects which the devil has always known how to put to the best use: pride and naïveté.

"And he [the serpent] said to the woman: Why hath God commanded you, that you should not eat of every tree of paradise? And the woman answered him, saying: Of the fruit of the trees that are in paradise we do eat: But of the fruit of the tree which is in the midst of paradise, God hath commanded us that we should not eat; and that we should not touch it, lest perhaps we die. And the serpent said to the woman: No, you shall not die the death. For God doth know that in what day soever you shall eat thereof, your eyes shall be opened: and you shall be as gods, knowing good and evil" (Gen. 3:1–5).

There is no "forbidden fruit" for the scientist or for those who benefit by his researches. Nothing hinders us from studying or from learning how better to use material things. They are ours; God has given them to us just as parents give bread to their children to eat, pictures to look at, sand to be played in.

But the grave fault of modern man lies in his imagining that because Nature has delivered over to him certain of her secrets, she will one day unveil all mysteries to him. He is mistaken in thinking that because he is now able to destroy some microbes and to make new machines, he will soon be able to eliminate all evil and secure all good; that he will end, in a word, by knowing all and by being able to do all, thus himself becoming "like God."

Our first parents at least left to the Creator a modest role, for they hoped to become no more than His rivals. Their nineteenth and twentieth-century descendants have gone far beyond them in pride and in naïveté. Certain of them have concluded that God is superfluous, and have therefore excluded Him. Others have cast doubt upon His existence, still other identify Him with the universe, His creation. Yet greater numbers relegate Him to a state so remote from the world that there is no longer any reason for thinking of Him at all. Thus has it come about that the God of Revelation has more and more disappeared from the schools, from homes and from the hearts of men.

This is what "naturalism" means: it is the negation of the supernatural, and it may be either theoretical or practical. The word does not indicate a body of homogeneous doctrine but rather a state of mind that believes only in those things apparent to the senses, that places all hope in visible nature, and is concerned only with things here below. It is a state of mind which has resulted in systems as diverse as atheism, agnosticism, pantheism, positivism, determinism, Marxism, existentialism, all of which have been — either in their turn or simultaneously — the vogue in the contemporary epoch.

Pride is hateful to God and carries its own punishment. Those who are filled with pride can no more escape that punishment than the two who dwelt in Eden. Blind to their last ends, the reality of the future life is hidden from their eyes. They have become enslaved to material

things, doomed to work and to sorrow without the hope
of compensation beyond the grave. Instead of going forward, they slide back to the state of the beasts, *jumenta
et pecora.* For, after all, is it not the sense of the divine
which more than anything else marks the distinction between man and the lower orders of creation? Is it not
by this that he has prevailed and does prevail against
them?

Now pride is the great sin of our time. It is said that
sin has nothing new about it, that it will always be. Yet
in the past even sinners remained in a certain sense religious, for they continued to recognize and to defer to
the Creator, even when they failed to obey Him. The
"prodigal sons" did not forget that they had a Father and
a home; they did not think themselves bound forever to
watch the swine and to eat with them. So it was that trust
in the Creator and remorse for sin finally made them set
out on the journey that led homeward. But the case of a
man who has lost the sense of the supernatural is grave in
another way. How can one who is uncertain of having a
soul feel the necessity of saving it? How can one to whom
eternity means nothingness exert himself to live in prep-
aration for that eternity?

And here, it seems, we find the reason for the frequent
apparitions of the Blessed Virgin in our time. It is because
of our blindness that she comes; it is the persistence and
increase of evil that have caused her to visit the earth so
often. What is more likely to cure us of false naturalism
than contact with what is above nature? Jesus appeared to
His disciples and even supped with them in order to convince them that He was risen indeed. It is in order to
reawaken our faith in the life to come that our heavenly Mother has, on more than fifty occasions, appeared

in living guise to her children in this world. For this reason
she has spoken to them, smiled, wept in their sight, caused
springs of water to flow from rock and earth; and it is
for this reason too that she has even left them as a pledge
her own portrait, engraved upon the Miraculous Medal.

How We Are to Read Our Lady's Message

But she has not stopped at healing our blindness, at
recalling to us our supernatural destiny; she is not satisfied
merely to show us our goal. She has wished to help us to
attain it by means fitted to the needs and exactions of our
time. Graces of every kind are contained in the message
which she has charged those who have seen her to deliver
to us. Therefore, in order to draw profit from it we must
read it aright and interpret it in the correct way.

Let us imagine that a traveler, passing by the farm
spoken of by St. Luke, finds no one there but a little boy
busily filling the troughs and he begins his message to the
child. In the evening the Prodigal Son returns from the
fields and is told of this visit; even hungrier than before, he
wails the whole afternoon.

"Do you say that this traveler came from my home and
that he has seen my father?" he asks the child.

"Exactly. And your father is still awaiting your return.
He grows sadder and sadder as he thinks that life is rushing by and that he may die before he sees you again."

"Is that all he said?"

"He added that your father is preparing the finest of
his calves so it may be ready for the feast when you return."

"Is that all?"

"Of course. What more do you wish? You understand

that I have not quoted his every word; for that matter, the traveler who passed by did not have much time to spend here. He was in a hurry to return to his own home, to his wife and children whom he has not seen for six months. He expressed his regret at not being able to wait for you, and galloped off on his horse. Anyway he said that no one will reproach you, that you are already forgiven, that the past will not even be mentioned, and that you ought to go home as soon as you can. He said this several times with the air of one who is feeling very happy at another's good fortune."

One may well believe that the Prodigal Son would pursue the subject no further, that he would not spend a week in asking for particulars about the appearance of the traveler, about his horse, or his hat, or seek to reconstruct what he had said down to the last iota. He would be in a transport of happiness, he would sing, he would quickly bring in his flock and would be gone within the hour, after having bidden farewell to his young companion.

It is well to act rather than to continue in endless debate. Also we should not waste our time in trifles when great things are at stake. There is no need for those who have seen the messenger to tell us all their secrets, nor is it necessary that they explain to us their heavenly visitor's every word and gesture. Is it for them to count her steps, to speak only in the most perfect theological terms, to say why the visitor came to this or to that place rather than to another? And if we find some obscurities, some trifling contradictions, some bizarre and even childish details in their accounts, let us recall that they are all really children, that they have not been gifted with inerrancy and the power of the Holy Ghost, that what they tell us is not on a par with the Scriptures.

Life is so short and the judgment is so near that we must hurry on. Instead of losing ourselves in what is insoluble and merely incidental, let us think of what is clear, of what is essential, and let us hasten to apply it for our best benefit. It would be to misunderstand and sadden the Virgin were we to see in her a Sphinx, a police officer, an accountant or a lawyer. She is a child of the earth who always speaks to us in our own tongue, a mother who calls to her children. What she expects is that her coming and her message be received with the loving and simple respect that any good son would show for the actions and words of his mother.

Nor does she wish us to think ourselves at a disadvantage if we cannot undertake the journey to Lourdes or to Fatima, or if it should happen that we break the chain of our Miraculous Medal. According to Catherine Labouré, the medal should be worn around the neck; yet Rochefort had his in his belt when it stopped the bullet from Cassagnac's pistol. She said, too, that the prayer to be said is: "O Mary, conceived without sin . . ." nevertheless, it was the *Memorare* that Ratisbonne prayed before his conversion.

Therefore, all that has been told us by those who have seen Our Lady or all they recommend is not of equal importance. In brief, Mary has not come among us in order to mystify us or to make our life darker and more troubled, but rather to enlighten us, encourage us, to help us, in a word, to save our souls.

Now we know well that we have no Saviour, no Master, other than Him who said: "I am the Good Shepherd . . . I am the Way, the Truth, and the Life. . . ." Consequently, the message of the Virgin is to be read in the light of His teaching.

Mary's message adds nothing to the Gospel, just as it takes nothing from it. Her message does not tell us anything new or sensational; it does not unveil the future of mankind, nor the date of the world's end, nor does it reveal any of those secrets that the Father did not will the Son to open before us. Still less does it destroy any of the exactions of the Gospel message, notably of those on which all else is based: "Wide is the way which leads to perdition . . . straight is the path which leads to life. . . . If any man would follow me, he must take up his cross . . . and take my yoke upon him."

We must not, therefore, seek in the message of the apparitions a way of finding dispensation from that yoke or from that cross, we must not expect it to show us some easy way to heaven. But we may seek and we will find in it an abundance of help that permits us to walk more courageously in the narrow path as we come to understand "how sweet is his yoke and how light is his burden," as the Saviour Himself has promised us.

Revelasti parvulis [2]

Some of the lessons of the Apparitions are unspoken for even before opening her lips Our Lady teaches us concerning several important matters.

Let us think, first of all, of the kind of collaborators she has selected; [3] they are all wanting in learning. Catherine in Paris, Mélanie and Maximin at La Salette, Bernadette

---

[2] *Abscondisti haec a sapientibus et revelasti ea parvulis . . .*
   I give thee thanks, O my Father, that thou hast hidden these things from the wise and has revealed them to little ones . . ."
                                                                    (Luke 10:21)
[3] We are not here concerned with Ratisbonne, for Our Lady neither spoke to him nor gave him any mission.

at Lourdes, the four children of Pontmain, the servant at Pellevoisin, the three children at Fatima, the five school children at Beauraing and the poor little girl at Banneux: here are eighteen people who would be unable, even were they to combine all their abilities, to write a letter without making mistakes, or to work out the simplest algebraic problem, or to name a noted clown or a celebrated actor.

Why did Mary not appeal instead to the learned to make known her message? To begin with she judged and wished to show that this was not necessary, just as Jesus showed us the same thing when He called the Apostles and founded His Church. And then it was doubtless evident to her that many of the learned are too pretentious, too lacking in simple directness, so that only a few of them could discharge so delicate a mission. She desired them and us to know this.

She seems to say that "they think they know everything because they have looked into some corners of the perishable earth, forgetting that many other parts of the physical universe, many suns revolving in space millions of light years away, still have to be probed. They think they know all that is to be known, and they are not even aware that it is God who has created all the planets and whose sustaining care holds them in space. They believe, moreover, in indefinite progress, as though their chemical and mechanical skills would ever be able to change human nature into something divine or angelic. To listen to them one might think they had already rebuilt the earthly paradise upon this planet, as if its people, in spite of their new labor-saving devices and means of pleasure, did not continue to complain and to behave as badly as ever. With their turn of mind how could they ever understand my message, which is spiritual? Even were they to grasp something of it, they would introduce so many corrections and add so many bizarre features that the message itself would become unrecognizable. Decidedly no, in thinking it over, these are not the ambassadors I seek. They would spoil everything."

Our Lady is certainly right about those scientists who have no faith, for who would entrust music to the deaf? Yet why did she also pass by the Christian scientists and not include even one well-educated person among her confidants? She was not prone to such exclusions in the past, and in former centuries she did, indeed, appear to more than one learned man. Has she then become unjust, and has she determined to look on all learning with horror because a certain kind of scientific outlook has encouraged unbelief? Is she like the mother who locks away all the knives in a drawer because her child has nearly cut off his finger?

Certainly this is not so. The most wise Virgin, *Virgo sapientissima*, does not condemn knowledge as such, nor does she condemn its good results. However, she does wish to turn us away from the idea that we may count on learning to solve the problem of our eternal destiny.

She seems to say: "See how well Catherine, Estelle, and these sixteen children have understood the great truths I came to recall and how carefully they have carried out their mission. They had no college degrees, any more than had St. Joseph, I myself, or many another saint in heaven. But they did have the foundation of a knowledge which is above that of worldly scholars, something which makes it possible for them to understand the past, the present and the future, things seen and unseen, God, angels and men, good and evil, pleasure and pain, the devil, the world and the flesh. However little they had, they knew whence they came and whither they were going; they

knew how to behave in the changing circumstances of life.
How often those who have more knowledge of the kind
the world holds in honor are beset and unhappy on earth,
and have little hope of gaining heaven.

"The knowledge prized by the world is like that water
which the Samaritan woman wearied of drawing from
Jacob's well, and of which Jesus said: 'Everyone who
drinks of this water will thirst again.' The knowledge of
the shepherds of La Salette and of the Sister of the poultry yard at Enghien is to be likened to that other water
of which He said: 'Who drinks of the water that I will
give him shall never thirst; but the water that I will give
him shall become in him a fountain of water springing up
unto life everlasting.' God gives some things to all unreservedly as He 'makes the sun shine upon the evil as well
as upon the good'; but there are other gifts He grants only
conditionally. So it is with the spiritual knowledge of which
I speak, and my Son told you of these conditions on the
day when 'He rejoiced in the Holy Spirit and said: I praise
thee Father, Lord of heaven and earth, that thou didst
hide these things from the wise and prudent, and have
revealed them to little ones. Yes, Father; for such was thy
good pleasure.' "

If we have no faith, these words show us how it is that
we may gain it; if we have faith, they tell us how we may
preserve it. We must remain *humble*, we must remain
little, if we are already so; we must become so, if we are
not. In other words, we must act in humility as is fitting
to creatures who are of themselves nothing. We must seek
from God alone those supernatural aids which we lack; we
must beg Him to grant them to us. He is always happy
to answer such prayers, for, as Jesus said: "What man is
there among you, who if his son asks him for a loaf will

hand him a stone; or if he asks for a fish, will hand him a serpent? If you, therefore, evil as you are, know how to give good gifts to your children how much more will your Father in heaven give good things to those who ask him!"

It is, after all, when we have received these "good things" that we will become wholly enlightened, whether we have been learned or ignorant before. Then it is that we shall know what is the one thing necessary; we shall understand that all truth is contained in Our Saviour's revelation. Having found *the Way*, we shall no longer look for guidance to those blind leaders who succeed each other generation after generation in offering to guide others, equally blind, with the result that all fall into the abyss.

Mammon, God of Riches

Another unspoken lesson to be gained from the apparitions has to do with money and the material things over which there is every reason to believe the Devil holds special and mysterious sway. Did not Jesus speak of the mammon of iniquity? Satan claims these things for his own, and he was not contradicted when he tempted Our Lord in the desert and, as the Gospel tells us, "having transported him to a high mountain showed him the kingdoms of this earth and said: 'to me they have been delivered, and to whomever I will I give them.' "

It is a fact, too, that Mary, over whom the demon has never prevailed, seems to hold money in horror and to wish to keep at a distance from anything that would recall it. None of those she selected to be her spokesmen had any money; four of them were actually in need: Estelle, Mélanie, Maximin and Mariette; the others were all poor.

Catherine had to borrow clothes in order to have the wardrobe required for her entry into the convent, and she left behind nothing but her prayer books when she died. If we were to add together all the possessions of those we have mentioned who were favored with visions of Our Lady we would not have enough today to buy a secondhand car. Nor did anyone among them grow rich as a result of what they had seen.

Why should it be that the rich, good as well as bad, seem to have been deliberately excluded from visitations from her who is the mother of all? When at Banneux Mariette asked her who she was, why did she at once reply: "I am the Virgin of the poor" — like a noble lady who at once mentions her descent lest she be mistaken for some plebeian of the same name? It is evident that this was to show that wealth is not a sign of true distinction, that poverty is in no way shameful, that for a Christian money should remain in the place assigned it in the Gospel, namely at the lowest rung in the scale of human values.

How fitting it is that this teaching be recalled to men in an age which knows so many willing servants of Mammon, when some of them even go so far as to assert that wealth is a sign of God's blessing. Were that so then neither Jesus nor his Mother was blessed of God, nor St. Joseph, St. Paul, St. Francis of Assisi, most of the other saints. We should have to say the same of a vast number of great writers and artists who have brought honor to the human race and left rich gifts to posterity but whose talents have not brought them success in the eyes of the world, i.e., in making money.

Rather than dwell on so manifest an absurdity, let us think of the words of Him to whom the Father has revealed all things and to whom the Father has committed the judgment of mankind. His words are terrifying to all those whether they be rich or poor, whose hearts and thoughts are centered on the acquisition of money:

"Accursed are you, ye rich, who have here on earth your consolation. . . . Blessed are the poor in spirit. . . ." It is madness to wish to be rich in the things of this world rather than to become so in the eyes of God. We have been warned that we must make a choice: "No man can serve two masters: you cannot serve God and mammon." And by the kind of bold hyperbole that is unforgettable, the Saviour adds that "it is as difficult for a rich man to enter into God's kingdom, as for a camel to go through the eye of a needle."

The difficulty is due, of course, to the fact that one can scarcely amass wealth without being guilty of injustice and cruelty; that zeal for the building up of a fortune leaves little time for thinking of one's soul; that wealth has a tendency to bind man to earth and makes it too easy for him to commit certain sins; that, in fine, wealth makes him so self-sufficient that he does not feel the need to cast himself into the arms of the Heavenly Father. It even becomes difficult for him to recite the *Pater Noster,* for why should a man who has enough to last for the next five years ask God for his "daily bread?" Why should he look forward to the coming of the kingdom, when he knows that, in Jesus' words, in God's kingdom the first shall be last and those that are filled with earth's delights shall go away hungry. Thus it is that certain rich men become atheists; for they are happy to think that there is no God and that the Gospel does not speak truly when it promises "weeping and gnashing of teeth" to the servants of mammon.

There is scarcely need to say that Our Lady no more

condemns the good rich man than she does the Christian
scholar; yet the fact that she keeps both at a distance
while drawing the poor closer to her is enough to indicate
that she looks on wealth as dangerous and the effort to
become rich as a risk not to be undertaken lightly. She
seems to say: Beware of the love of money; remember how
it is accursed by my Son. If He has done so, it is because
it was needful, for He loves rather to bless than to curse;
but since there is greater difficulty in being good than in
being evil when one is rich, it were better to choose the
safer course and to seek more earnestly to save your immortal soul than to pile up treasures that will perish.

The Woman and the Serpent

Having considered those who saw Our Lady, we will
pass to the visions themselves, and will note that they have
varied according to time and place. Nor have they shown
the Blessed Virgin identical in age, facial appearance, or
in her dress. However, she has always presented herself
under the aspect of a real woman, a woman described
and praised in Sacred Scripture, a woman such as men are
happy to have as a mother, such as they hope to find as a
wife. She is indeed far from that new anthropological spe-
cies, a compound of actress, clothes-horse and virago,
neither male nor female, certain of whom we see about
us today.

As she is described by those who have seen her the
woman of the apparition is elegantly but decently dressed.
Her gown reaches to her feet; her head is covered by a
veil, her clear voice is low, her face unpainted. She
keeps her reserve and her mystery; her walk, her gestures,
her voice, her smile are all sweet, harmonious and chaste.

Reserved and modest, she both attracts and arouses respect; seemingly weak, she yet dominates.

There is little doubt that the Virgin wished to give a lesson in modesty to those women who claim to be Christians but whose appearance belies the claim. A lesson in femininity is also found herein for the "boyish" women of the day who may now perhaps realize how their behavior has cost them the God-given gift of reigning over the hearts of men. . . .

All those who saw the visions of Our Lady were enraptured. At La Salette and Banneux they could speak only of "the lovely Lady"; Catherine Labouré wrote: "she was more beautiful than I can ever tell"; Bernadette described her as "young and beautiful, especially beautiful, so beautiful that I have never seen anyone like her"; and the children of Fatima declared that the Blessed Virgin was "so beautiful that we were blinded and had often to lower our eyes."

To this perfection of physical beauty is joined the unspotted purity of her whom we call the Immaculate Conception. It was by this title that Our Lady spoke of herself at Lourdes and at Beauraing, as she had previously asked that this name be engraved on the Miraculous Medal. We know that she wished to be portrayed here with her foot on the serpent of evil. God had promised that it would be she who would gain this victory: "And the Lord said to the serpent: Because thou hast done this thing, thou art cursed . . . I will put enmities between thee and the woman . . . her seed shall crush thy head . . ." (Gen. 3:14–15).

Thus are evoked two truths apart from which no one can hope to know very much either of the nature of man or of world history: the existence of original sin and the intervention of the Devil in earthly affairs. "The spirit is willing, but the flesh is weak," said Jesus. And St. Paul avowed that he found two men within himself. It is because of original sin that a dual nature exists in us; this explains our weakness, our ignorance, our lack of will, our perverse and unworthy leanings, our falls and our unhappiness.

Many in our age place little faith in this belief, treat man as though he were wholly good and inaccessible to evil influences. This age surrounds man with all conceivable occasions of sin, and lulls him with the illusion that by means of laboratory experiments and technology he will one day attain to perfect happiness, and in this world!

How pleasing it must be to Satan to see thus rooted out of the human heart the religious yearnings and the longing for heaven that were fostered even by primitive religions. The Devil is also well pleased that he is allowed to pass unremarked for he has greater power to do evil when he is undisturbed. Who nowadays is worried about Satan? Who would dare mention his name in one of those magazines or newspapers from which the majority of our contemporaries draw the basis of their culture and spiritual outlook? Nevertheless, it is no myth that this evil spirit "for whom God has prepared everlasting flames" wanders like a roaring lion among us, seeking whom he may devour.

Jesus warned us to be on our guard against Satan's malice, as well as against the evil propensities of our fallen nature: "Watch and pray that you may not enter into temptation, He says: be as wise as the serpent. . . ." Cut off an arm or pluck out an eye if it be for the good of your soul. . . . Could He have told us any more plainly that many worldly fulfilments are poison to us; that we ought not wish to try everything, to taste everything, to see everything, but that sacrifice and renunciation should continue to play great roles in our lives?

By means of these apparitions Our Lady reminds those of us who have lost sight of these words of Our Saviour, and who are tempted to dream of a Christianity without the cross, that we must always "do penance," that we must "bear our cross." And this is not only "because the disciple is no greater than his master," but because we will never be able to put Satan to flight or to conquer our natural leanings toward evil by relying merely on technical progress.

Mary, the Mother of God

This is a hard saying. One of Our Lord's disciples told Him that His words fell harshly on his ears. We might feel inclined to say as much to Our Lady in respect to some of the lessons she gives us and the illusions she takes away. Does she not, after all, offer a program that is dreary and discouraging when she demands that we be humble, that we distrust wealth, that we mortify our senses, that we strive against our nature and do battle with Satan to the very moment of our death?

Our Lord's disciples, too, lost courage at times. When He spoke of the eye of the needle and the camel, the Gospel tells us they wondered greatly and said among themselves: "Who then can be saved?" Jesus looked at them and said: "With men this is impossible but with God all things are possible." Now the disciples had earlier heard him say: "My Father and I are one," and they knew that their Master's power was the power of God. This thought reassured and comforted them.

We too may take courage from this, for we know that Our Lord is all powerful, and that He places His power at Mary's disposal. This is a truth upon which she most often insists: "I am the mistress of my Son's heart; He loves me so much that He can refuse me nothing." So she said at Pellevoisin. And at La Salette she declared: "Ah, if you knew what it costs me to withhold his avenging arm." It is costly; she must sometimes plead, but in the end she always prevails. Her prayers are infallible because there is no saint in heaven who prays as she does and because He to whom she prays is her Son. "I am the Mother of the Saviour," were her words at Beauraing and again at Banneux.

When she was seen in the Rue du Bac she wore rings adorned with precious stones that sent forth rays of light. "These lights," said she, "symbolize the graces I give to those who ask for them." And when Catherine noted with astonishment that there were also stones which seemed to lack fire, she explained that they too would dispense their light if more people sought for grace. Her Son is so generous and she herself so dowered with gifts that she scarcely knows what to do with them. It seems as if she said: "How sad it is to wear these precious stones that Catherine thinks are false, how sad to hold these graces that are unused. I wish to give them to men. . . . But to whom? . . . Why do not all who need them ask for them? . . ."

At Pellevoisin she suddenly brought down rain in Estelle's room to show her, as she said, "the grace that I will pour down upon those who wear the scapular." And there fell an abundant shower, of which each drop represented a grace. Here again she wished to show how much is lost by those who do not ask.

"I will convert sinners," she said at Banneux, and the examples of Ratisbonne and the Abbé de Pradt show that a moment is enough for her to convert even the most recalcitrant. Conversion, which assures everlasting bliss to the soul, is evidently what the mother of men can best obtain for them; but she also procures temporal favors for her clients. All that can allay human suffering or give new courage is at her disposal.

At Pontmain she promised to turn back the Prussians, and on the following night she barred the way to the army of General von Schmidt. At La Salette, she affirmed her power to change rocks into heaps of grain. The chronicles of Lourdes and of the Miraculous Medal tell of so many cures of illness that we know she can prevail against them all. It is only wealth, worldly honors and pleasures that she does not seem to grant. "I do not promise to make you happy on earth," she said to Bernadette, "but I will do so in heaven."

The Gospel teaches us that Jesus was perfectly obedient to his Mother while He was on earth. The apparitions provide an opportunity for Mary to show us that He continues to be so in heaven and so her own power is always the same. If we seek to know its extent, the story of the wedding at Cana has much to tell.

St. John records that toward the close of the banquet the wine ran out. Was this because too little had been provided, or because the guests had partaken of it too copiously? Our Lady was touched, feeling for the embarrassment of the one side and the disappointment of the other. She leaned toward Jesus and whispered: "They have no more wine." "What is that to you and to me?" was His only reply. So much the worse for those who have made the mistake; let them repair the error, if they can. As for me, I can do nothing, "My hour has not yet come;" and perhaps it is not my Father's will that I anticipate it. St. John, in fact, plainly states that "up to this time, Jesus had wrought no miracles." Nevertheless, the Evangelist goes on to tell us, this conversation was barely over when Mary turned to the servants and said: "Do whatever He tells you." Now there were six stone jars for the Jewish ceremony of purification, each with a capacity of between two and three measures, a measure in Galilee being equivalent to ten gallons. Jesus spoke to the servants and ordered them to fill these urns with water and they filled them to the brim. Then he said: "Draw out now, and take to the chief steward." This they did, and when the steward had tasted this wine he questioned the bridegroom as to whence it came. "Every man," he said, "at first sets forth the good wine, and when they have drunk freely [and whose palates are no longer so sensitive to taste] then that which is poorer. But thou hast kept the good wine till now."

Nothing better shows Mary's limitless power. She was aware of it, because although the miracle she suggested seemed refused to her, she knew, nonetheless, that it would take place; and she bade the servants to carry out her Son's commands. But what is so striking is the way in which Jesus obeys. He does not even wait for an express request; a mere suggestion suffices and He immediately changes His plans; he upsets his own time table and, in place of a little ordinary wine, He provides a hundred and fifty gallons of the very best.

It was no exaggeration for Mary to describe herself as "mistress of the heart" of the Saviour. When he is ready to punish us, she "withholds His arm"; when He remains aloof from us for the very best of reasons, she intervenes in our favor. We might almost say that she causes Him to exceed the bounds of His own goodness, did we not know that this goodness is infinite, and that it is His good pleasure that she forces, so to speak, His hand.

Mary, Mother of Men

Is it not characteristic of a mother to risk everything for the good of her children? No one knows better than Our Saviour that Mary is our Mother, for it was He who gave her to us on Calvary. One of the last things he did was to say, "Woman, behold thy Son," as he pointed to St. John. Christians have always believed that at that moment John was the representative of all humanity. Thenceforth, we have had to love us the incomparable Mother whose heart God had formed so that it might love Jesus. And she, made one with Him, like Him desires our salvation and shares in the sufferings He underwent for our redemption.

The apparitions show that Mary showers upon us all the love and care with which she surrounded Our Lord while he was on earth. How like a mother she is to those to whom she appears. We seem to hear her saying to Catherine's angel: "Take the form of a five-year-old child so that she will not be frightened. . . . Awaken her gently. . . . Be careful to make the passage light enough for her to see her way. . . ." And, as she receives the novice in the chapel, we seem to hear her say: "So you wished to see me? . . . Come closer . . . come near me, rest against me; put your hands on my knees; do not fear to rumple the silk of my robe: I have others. . . ." And after an hour and a half of this nearness: "Now are you satisfied, wholly satisfied? . . . Ah, it is well. . . . *Au revoir,* good night! Do not

stumble as you return . . . I have told the angel to light
you on your way back."

Nor did she fail to say "good night" and *au revoir* to
little Mariette Beco. She read the letter that Estelle Faguette wrote to her, and she paid seventeen visits to her
lonely sickroom. She showed her heart to the school
children of Beauraing so that they were able to see that
"her heart is of gold." She spoke in their native dialect
to the shepherds of La Salette, and seated herself on the
little pile of stones they had prepared for her. She put
them all at ease from the very beginning, for she did not
want anyone who saw her to be afraid. "Fear not," she
said when she first came into their sight. She spoke to
them of things interesting to them; she patiently explained
the mission she wished to entrust to them; she whispered
into their ears a little secret for themselves alone. Above
all, she smiled on them; she smiled even when Bernadette
sprinkled holy water as an exorcism. She smiled on all
that smile that reveals the greatest kind of human love,
for it is the love of a mother for her child. One is reminded
of Isaiah's words: "You shall be carried at the breasts,
and upon the knees they shall caress you. As one whom
the mother caresseth, so will I comfort you . . ." (Isa.
66:12–13). And so, how great was their joy whenever she
returned! They were in ecstasy as long as she remained
with them; nothing could restrain them from hurrying to
the place where she had promised to be; they would have
gone on their knees to the ends of the earth to follow her.
And how dreadful was their desolation when she said that
she would not return! . . . They were no longer the same
as they had been; henceforth they would be wholly different, for their whole souls had been transmuted during
the brief time they had felt themselves loved with such

perfection of love, and of this it was that they thought for the rest of their lives.

From the story of the apparitions we derive the same impressions as were given to those who saw the heavenly visitor; for we feel, as they did, that we are really her children. It was not just for nine among the French, six among the Belgians, and three among the Portuguese that Mary appeared, but for all those loved and ransomed by her divine Son. As a matter of fact, she came less to reassure those who saw her that she is their Mother than to charge them to remind us that she is ours. She said to them repeatedly they were to become messengers: "All that you have heard and seen you are to tell to all; tell them of my smile, of my tears; of my reproaches, my counsels, my promises, my message. In a word tell *these things to all my people;* spread these medals and these scapulars abroad that virtue may come forth just as it did from the Saviour's robe when it was touched by the woman suffering from an issue of blood. Point out to the entire world these springs that gush forth graces at all seasons, this grotto, this mountain, this little wood."

There are no supernatural happenings more in accord with the Gospel than the apparitions of Our Lady. They exemplify its teaching in a most wonderful manner, for as everyone knows its basis is love. The relations of Creator and creature are not governed by the laws of human compatibility; it is rather love that rules, and that has the final word. It was love which moved God to create us and to concern Himself with our fate and our well being; love likewise that impelled Jesus to sacrifice Himself for us upon the Cross. Our love makes answer to this divine love; it is displayed in faith, in trust, in thanksgiving, in patience, prayer and brotherly love, and it strives to accomplish the divine will. Thus may we share in that peace promised by the angels on Christmas night to men of good will.

Yet there are times when trouble and discouragement press heavily upon us, when we feel broken by trials, surrounded by misgivings, made victims of our own weakness. These are the moments when there resound in man's ears those fearsome words of Love condemned: "I will hide my face from them, and will consider what their last end shall be: for it is a perverse generation, and unfaithful children" (Deut. 32:20).

In such times how much comfort shall we find in recalling these appearances of Our Lady and her pledges of universal motherhood. Since God has made Mary the new Eve and truly *the Mother of the living*, there are no real orphans, there is no ground for despair; rather is there ground for hope that an appeal may be made from the very sentence pronounced by God. Can a mother ever forget her child, can she ever cease to love him? Does he ever become an object from which she turns away? On the contrary, it is to the most wretched of her children that she manifests her tenderest love. None then will be lost among those who place their hope in Our Lady and who pray to her. The apparitions prove her as bound to the great human family as was Jehovah to the people chosen of old:

"He found him in a desert land, in a place of horror, and of vast wilderness: he led him about, and taught him: and he kept him as the apple of his eye.

"As the eagle enticing her young to fly, and hovering over them, he spread his wings, and hath taken him and carried him on his shoulders" (Deut. 32:10–11).